S O N G
OF THE NIGHTINGALE

Also by Michael Ford

published by Paulist Press

FATHER MYCHAL JUDGE
An Authentic American Hero

Other Titles
not published by Paulist Press

WOUNDED PROPHET
ETERNAL SEASONS
DISCLOSURES

S O N G
OF THE NIGHTINGALE

A Modern Spiritual Canticle

Michael Ford

Paulist Press
New York/Mahwah, N.J.

Quotations from the psalms are from the Taizé translations, available online at www.sogang.ac.kr/~anthony/psalms/, selected and arranged for singing and meditation by Brother Anthony of Taizé. Unless otherwise noted, all other scripture quotations outlined herein are from the New Revised Standard Version, copyright © 1989 by the Division of Christian Education of the National Council of Churches of Christ in the United States of America. Used by permission. All rights reserved.

Cover design by Trudi Gershenov
Book design by Lynn Else

Illustration page xii, Jesus Christ blessing, 18th century, Wologda (N. Russia). Copyright © 1997 The Trustees of Glenstal Abbey. All rights reserved. Photograph © 1997 Michael Blake.

Library of Congress Cataloging-in-Publication Data

Ford, Michael, 1956-
   Song of the nightingale : a modern spiritual canticle / Michael Ford.
     p. cm.
   Includes bibliographical references.
   ISBN 0-8091-4335-6 (alk. paper)
   1. Ford, Michael, 1956- 2. Christian biography—Great Britain. I. Title.
   BR1725.F5455A3 2005
   274.1'0825'092—dc22

                        2004024929

Published by Paulist Press
997 Macarthur Boulevard
Mahwah, New Jersey 07430

www.paulistpress.com

Printed and bound in the
United States of America

To the memory of my grandparents

As prophets, our vocation is to seek out the words of God which are hidden within each thing, from stone to angel. By these divine words or *logoi* God brought each thing into existence and keeps it in existence, and gives it its unique role in the cosmic symphony.

BROTHER AIDAN

The Church is always renewed from the edges rather than the center.

ARCHBISHOP ROWAN WILLIAMS

CONTENTS

PART THREE
Living Flame

THE CALLING

There is a time
for flying from the nest
to know the joy of freedom
in the faithful quest
of winging from the known
to unknown places.

There is a time
for ambiguity and pain,
a time to prize the light
in tear-filled eyes
to share the darkness
shading other faces.

There is a time
for nightingales to sing
when evening shadows fall
and death wings loved ones
to unique completion
and eternal graces.

Harry Wiggett
Specially composed for
Song of the Nightingale

PRELUDE

My book is the whole visible creation before me...whenever I wish to read in it the words of God.

ANTHONY THE GREAT

*A*s the dawn chorus grows faint, my bleary eyes begin to focus on *The Icon of Christ*. This is the first image I see in the morning and is a daily reminder of a visit I made to the Benedictine Abbey of Glenstal in the west of Ireland. It was there I encountered the original. The Russian icon, part of a unique collection in the crypt, shows Christ as the Pantokrator or ruler of all things. This, of course, is a traditional Byzantine theme, but it is intriguing to discover how the Russian church reinterpreted Christ's power as the manifestation of his compassion. His being is kenotic, or self-emptying. The Son of God divests himself of power and glory in becoming human, veiling his divine majesty in the form of a humble, suffering servant. This theology underpins my spiritual understanding of vocation.

The green-and-golden-hued icon signifies that Christ has not only shared our human condition, with all its pains and joys, but has also opened up for us the possibility of seeing God. I have looked into those gentle, penetrating eyes many times but have never felt judged. As Christ blesses, he holds a book displaying a text from the Gospel of St. Matthew: "Come to me, all you that are weary and are carrying heavy burdens, and I will give you rest. Take my yoke

1

upon you, and learn from me; for I am gentle and humble in heart, and you will find rest for your souls. For my yoke is easy, and my burden is light."

According to a monk, both the scriptural text and the icon itself stress "the accessibility of God in Christ, his drawing near to us in mercy, and the power of his love for all creation: hence the tender compassion of this face, its luminous sensitivity and its power to fascinate those who pray before it."[1] Many have testified to the icon's healing power. A modern mystic from Switzerland, Joa Bolendas, says anyone contemplating this icon "begins to be oriented spiritually toward Christ and his light. Thus you receive light and spiritual strength. What happens then is most holy."[2]

When I first saw this image of loving humility, entitled *Jesus Christ Blessing,* I felt compelled to buy a postcard reproduction and bring it home. I knew instinctively that it held meaning for me. I framed the picture and placed it on a yew table, beside a dumpy white candle. Behind the icon I placed a specially carved wooden box containing olive oil from the Holy Land. I asked a hospital chaplain to bless the balm. I sometimes use it in private acts of prayer with those who are suffering. *The Icon of Christ* reminds me that "the glory of Jesus does not come from the power of the world, but is a reflection of another world, the realm of the Holy Trinity..." where there is "no trace of selfish grasping, no desire to dominate or control others." The persuasive power of love "simply suffers, but by suffering, it shines."[3] In front of the icon, I place photographs of friends who are sick, as well as pictures of those who have recently died—people as well as animals (family pets among them).

For me, the icon symbolizes a unique vocation. It not so much embraces but blesses the ambiguities that make me the person I am: my priestly and journalistic temperaments; my Anglo-Catholicism and my Roman Catholicism. Sometimes I sit in front of the icon and try to make sense of these paradoxes. Then I remember that Thomas Merton felt that the very contradictions in his life were, to some extent, signs of God's mercy to him. In a source of insecurity, he found the greatest security. Merton said that all life tended to grow in mystery, inscaped with paradox and contradiction, yet centered, in its very heart, on the divine mercy.

Many centuries ago, the great spiritual teacher Meister Eckhart said that the deepest truth of God was to be found in paradox. As a Benedictine commentator notes, Eckhart "keeps us perpetually swinging from one pole to the other; he will not let us rest in either. To rest in one and forget the other is to lose hold of the truth which is essentially paradoxical." Having made a statement, Eckhart "will often go on to deny it; but the truth lies neither in the affirmation nor in the denial, but in the tug-of-war between the two." The purpose of paradox is to "bring the normal human intellect to the awareness of its own limitations, and thus open it up to the possibility of a higher kind of knowing."[4] When people understandably seek clarification as to whether or not I am an Anglican or a Roman Catholic, if I am on the side of the media or on the side of the church, or whether I think I should really have been ordained, I can only point to the paradox.

The writer and Episcopal priest Elizabeth Canham goes as far as to say that accepting paradox is a necessary aspect of spiritual growth:

> Embracing ambiguity means giving up the myth that one day we will have it all together and everything will become clear. As long as we are on this earth we will be subject to the confusions, the paradoxes and unsolved questions which are an inevitable accompaniment of being human. This does not mean that we have somehow got onto the wrong track; rather it indicates that we have opted for reality with all its frustrations and possibilities, instead of clinging to simplistic explanations and

rigid structures. It means that, like Jeremiah, we have chosen life.[5]

In his painting *The Calling of the Apostles Peter and Andrew*—a print from the National Gallery of Art in Washington hangs in my room near the Russian icon—the great Italian artist Duccio di Buoninsegna shows the brothers like twins, "a single apostolate with two dimensions."[6] This insight is helpful in understanding "the companionship" that exists between my respective dual vocations which have been lived out on the edge of the church, just as Christ calls Peter and Andrew from the shoreline. Yet for all their togetherness and compatibility, there is also aloneness and an uncomfortable sense of difference. As I am still learning, vocation and vulnerability are inseparable in the particularity of a calling—and this is where the nightingale flies in: The bird that sings in the dark calls each of us to claim a uniqueness that has been divinely bestowed. Just as I look into the eyes of *The Icon of Christ,* so I listen out for the song of the nightingale. The one confers my vocation, the other proclaims it.

A summer visitor to parts of North West Europe, the nightingale *(luscinia megarhynchos)* is a shy creature that rarely makes public appearances away from the undergrowth of deciduous woodlands, coppiced heaths, and thickets bordering rivers and ponds. Its other desired haunts are bushes on the edges of damp, overgrown parks, gardens, and hillsides. With its long reddish tail, frequently held in a cocked position, the bird is invariably solitary, more often heard than seen. Acclaimed for its richness and quality, the song of the nightingale is unique. It has many fast and joyously bubbling phrases and repetitions, exquisite in variety and tune, especially the low, sustained notes that it delivers from dense cover. The tonal ambit ranges from deep, opulent sequences to the purest of treblelike trills and flourishes; from throaty chuckles to long-range whistles. Bird watchers say you cannot easily confuse the nightingale with other songbirds, yet its repertoire often includes melodies learned in the woods. The voice of the nightingale, heard solo at dead of night, comes through the clear, warm, early-summer air as one of the most delightful birdsongs in the world. But the song period is short, spanning only the second half of May and June. In the undergrowth much of what you can hear is the "chack" and "churr" noises with which the nightingale deters intruders from its place of concealment. Yet, as soon as the young are hatched out, the bird loses its beautiful voice and schools its young with a harsh, raucous call.[7]

One explanation for nightingales spending much of their time out of view is that the males migrate several days in advance of the females. On arrival, they set up territories that they defend by song. They are said to sing to the night skies to attract the females passing overhead. But this theory does not account for the fact that all these species continue their nocturnal singing until well into the breeding season.

Many legends encircle the bird but all emanate from the fanciful suggestion that the bird sings with its breast pressed against a sharp thorn to keep itself awake. According to mythology, the nightingale originally had only one eye and stole the single eye of the slow worm. Since then, the worm has since been searching for the bird in order to regain its sight. So the nightingale sings all night to keep alert to the possibility of a reprisal attack.

I first became aware of the nightingale's spiritual significance when I was a theology student, writing essays long into the night. As part of a course in Christian mystical writings, we had to analyze the work of the sixteenth-century Spanish priest St. John of the Cross. One of the texts was the *Spiritual Canticle,* a love poem about the soul searching for the divine. It is devised as a romantic dialogue between bridegroom (God) and bride (the soul):

Bridegroom: The small white dove
                    Has returned to the ark with an olive
                        branch;
                    And now the turtledove
                    Has found its longed-for mate
                    By the green river banks.

                    She lived in solitude,
                    And now in solitude has built her nest;
                    And in solitude He guides her,
                    He alone, Who also bears
                    In solitude the wound of love.

Bride: Let us rejoice, Beloved,
                    And let us go forth to behold ourselves
                        in Your beauty,
                    To the mountain and to the hill,
                    To where the pure water flows,
                    And further, deep into the thicket.

                    And then we will go on
                    To the high caverns in the rock
                    Which are so well concealed;
                    There we shall enter
                    And taste the fresh juice of the
                        pomegranates.

                    There You will show me
                    What my soul has been seeking,
                    And then You will give me,
                    You, my Life, will give me there
                    What You gave me on that other day:

                    The breathing of the air,
                    The song of the sweet nightingale,
                    The grove and its living beauty

In the serene night,
With a flame that is consuming and
painless.[8]

In his commentary, John of the Cross explains that, through the "breathing of the air," the soul hears the sweet voice of her beloved calling to her. She expresses "her delightful jubilation and calls both voices the song of the nightingale." The mystic goes on to say:

Just as the nightingale begins its song in the spring, once the wintry cold, rain, and changes have passed, and provides melody for the ear and refreshment for the spirit, so in this actual communication and transformation of love which the bride has now attained in this life, in which she is freed from and protected against all temporal disturbances and changes, and divested and purged of imperfections, penalties, and clouds in the senses and the spirit, she feels a new spring, in spiritual freedom and breadth, and gladness. She hears the sweet song of her Bridegroom Who is her sweet nightingale. Renewing and refreshing the substance of the soul with the sweetness and mellowness of His voice, He calls her as He would call one now disposed to make the journey to eternal life, and she hears this pleasant voice: *Arise, make haste, my love, my dove, my beautiful one, and come; for now the winter has passed, the rains have gone far off, the flowers have appeared in our land, the time of pruning has come, and the voice of the turtledove is heard in our land.* [Song 2:10–12][9]

The song of the nightingale invites us to look for the extraordinary in the ordinary. This is, of course, what journal-

ists do. But the spiritual implications are more far-reaching.
We may think we are very ordinary people with few extraordinary gifts. But the symbol of the nightingale reminds us that,
in and through the ordinariness of our lives, God can accom-
plish extraordinary things. As a spiritual guide once told me:
"Be yourself but make that self all that God wants it to be."

All my life I have sensed within me the stirrings of a
vocation rather than the makings of a career. I have a nonlin-
ear approach to my life and work. I am a "both-and" rather
than an "either-or" person. Therefore, discerning the precise
nature of the calling and trying to convince others of its
uniqueness have not always been easy. I once found particular encouragement in the words of a Dominican preacher
who described Christ's ministry as "painfully slow...a
process of discovery on the part of Jesus quite as much as on
the part of the disciples...the story of a man searching, and
not immediately finding, what it is that he is for."

I was baptized and confirmed within the catholic tradition of the Church of England. During my twenties, when I
was working as a newspaper journalist in the English
provinces, I started thinking seriously about becoming an
Anglican priest, but a few years later decided to be received
into the Roman Catholic Church. But I could not settle, nor
could I bring myself to be reconfirmed. The following year I
went off to the university to study theology and discovered,
in a new enlightened climate of intellectual thinking, that
denominations really didn't matter that much.

Then, three years after graduating, while working as a
BBC news producer for a large city radio station, a drunk
driver crashed into my car and nearly claimed my life. The
vehicle was a write-off but I remained intact. As I rested my
head on the steering wheel and gave thanks for my survival,
I knew that, somehow, the accident would be a turning point
or, perhaps more accurately, a catalyst. At that time I was
drinking from both streams of Christendom and was tenta-
tively reexploring the idea of Anglican priesthood again.

Reporting on the search for a missing schoolgirl (later found raped and murdered) affected me deeply. As I covered the story day by day, my heart reached out to the anxious parents standing with the police teams on the other side of the street. With a microphone in my hand and a radio car mast behind me, I often felt like abandoning my broadcast and walking over to console the family in a more priestly way. But I was still uneasy about officially going forward for ordination because institutional priesthood seemed to me to be more about power than love—the antithesis of *The Icon of Christ*. I was also influenced by the words of an Anglican solitary, Maggie Ross, who writes in *Pillars of Flame: Power, Priesthood, and Spiritual Maturity* that "ordination does *not* bestow the humility of Christ, which is priesthood."[10] And I liked the way she dedicated this book to four people "two ordained, two not, all true priests."

Whatever the calling was, I knew it could not be contained by any one denomination. Perhaps my vocation was to be a prototype for a new form of priesthood. During my convalescence, I decided to reevaluate my understanding of ministry and keep a spiritual journal as a disciplined form of discernment. After all, it seemed only apposite that a journalist, who probed other people and proclaimed their stories, should occasionally have the willpower to question and report his own, albeit privately. As I ventured into the interior and began to jot things down, I found myself unearthing spiritual resources to help me become the person God *really* intended me to be. But I sensed it would be a long and arduous journey. As the Jesuit priest and Third Order Franciscan William Hart McNichols has pointed out, there is a sacred and unique nature to each individual's priesthood that takes years to unravel. Far from being a persona or outfit that one puts on and takes off, this form of priesthood corresponds more to the ancient image of a sacramental seal on the soul and cannot be shed. From Christ comes the wounding of the call and the continued wounding of humility to keep the call alive. Vocation involves vulnerability and suffering. McNichols even goes as far as to say that, if we do not find suffering in ourselves, then we must seek it out in order to become authentic spiritual beings.

This, then, is a journalist's inside story, spun from the threads of my spiritual reportage and chronicled largely as it was originally written. Edited and reworked for publication, the entries cover a period of thirteen years. Although there is an underlying melody, I have occasionally reordered the original sequences to vary the rhythm. The vicissitudes of my inner life seem to resemble a war correspondent's diary at times as mood swings kick in. The extracts are honed from notes I scribbled down when I was musing along the shoreline, up a mountain, through a wood, or across a wilderness (both physically and metaphorically). As you will discover, the presence of nature has both stilled and permeated my restlessness. There is a blend of short extracts and more discursive pieces, along with quotations from spiritual thinkers and conversations with fellow pilgrims who have had to work out what vocation means for them in a range of different situations. A break between sequences indicates a new journal entry, written on a subsequent day.

I must admit to being a little nervous about revealing so much of my own journey in this way, but I trust the uniqueness of this story will connect with your own, for as Henri Nouwen writes: "What is experienced as most unique often proves to be most solidly embedded in the common condition of being human."[11] It might also encourage you to search for the extraordinary in the ordinary wherever you happen to be. The Dominican writer Paul Murray suggests that, like Jonah, "we need, in the spiritual life, to be shocked and shaken out of certain fixed ways of thinking and feeling. We need to begin to recognize God in places where we would never, perhaps, have suspected his presence before, and not only in the big city or in the places of our enemies, but also in the seemingly banal and bizarre circumstances of our lives."[12]

After the publication of my first book, a reader wrote to explain how the telling of that particular story had released "something in me to be my true self." I can only hope that the sharing of this spiritual canticle might unleash in you a deeper sense of vocation to become the person God intends you to be, a song that may have lain dormant for years but longs to break out.

The Quantocks
August 2004

PART ONE
Whistling Breezes

1

VENTURING WITHIN

*Stand at the crossroads, and look; ask for the
ancient paths, ask where the good way is; and
walk in it...*

JEREMIAH 6:16

*I*t is a time for reimagining. I find myself philosophiz-
ing under the shade of the Atlantic palms. Had it not
been for the accident, I doubt I would be sitting here on a
breezy hotel terrace listening to the beguiling waves on the
other side of a tropical shrubbery. I keep reliving that
December night....The drunk driver crashing into the back of
my car at high speed, my seat belt being torn from its mount-
ings, the impact causing me to careen down a busy street as
other vehicles swerved to avoid me. I managed to brake,
coming to an abrupt halt in the middle of a four-way junc-
tion. I knew the car was scrunched up so I gingerly glanced
down to check the state of my own bodywork. I couldn't see
any blood or bits of bone, but started to worry about internal injuries.

Then a face appeared at the window. It was none other
than the inebriated driver slurring his words into an apology,
checking I was still alive. I couldn't open the door but,
through the glass, asked him if he was all right. He nodded
and got back into his car, which then swayed from side to
side as he sped off. He was later forced off the road by a fire

engine and subsequently jailed because he had already lost his license for a previous drunk-driving offence.

Miraculously my only injury was a painful whiplash, which is keeping me off work for a couple of months. To recuperate I have flown to the Canary Islands, a volcanic archipelago off the west coast of Africa. Some historians believe the legendary continent of Atlantis was located here—and the ships of Christopher Columbus stopped here on their way to discover the New World. I feel that, by embarking on this journal, I am beginning a spiritual odyssey. I will be committing to paper thoughts and feelings I have never had the energy to articulate before. The last thing a journalist wants to do after an exhausting shift is to write, so I have never broached this style of concentrated recollection before. But I am sure this is where the *real* stories lie. With the accident occurring at a time when I am oscillating about becoming a priest, there are many depths to plumb. In my more spectacular reveries, I even wonder if I have been spared for a purpose. Although I am more comfortable reporting other people's stories, this kind of focused writing is helping me unravel my own mysteries. As Elizabeth Canham puts it: "The journal helps us take the road inward and so to discover who we really are. As we write, the ambiguity of human experience with its hidden desires and impulses is revealed. Our questions increase and need to be explored, not so much to resolve them as to place them in the context of the mystery at the heart of the universe."[13]

My pilgrimage through life is spiritual and journalistic at the same time. These two aspects of one personality overlap, often deftly, but sometimes awkwardly. In some people's eyes, the dissimilarities are so blatant they are simply irreconcilable—I cannot serve God and mammon. It is true that the church and the media are sometimes perceived as archenemies and even rival institutions of power—indeed, at their worst, both can be breeding grounds for envy and resentment. But I have always thought that their offspring, spiritu-

ality and journalism, are much more like cousins, even sib-
lings, searching for truth and justice in their own distinctive
ways. Strange as it may sound, I have always felt called to be
a journalist—in a priestly sense. It's not a vocation the church
would necessarily acknowledge. I have been wrestling with
this conundrum for a long time now. But as well as the conflicts, there has also been maturation and, I believe, a unity
at the heart of the struggle.

So which is the real me? Where do I really belong?
These are questions we all have to confront at different times
in our lives. Time and again, I have pondered the words of
Dietrich Bonhoeffer (written from his cell in Nazi Germany)
and applied them to my own dilemma:

> Who am I? This or the other?
> Am I one person today and tomorrow another?
> Am I both at once?[14]

Perhaps this journal will help me unravel the puzzle.
The drunk driver is in jail, thousands of miles from the freedom of these Spanish islands where the wild brown canary
still sings in the fields and forests. There is so much fleeting
beauty here, but I can't help wondering what story is breaking back home in the newsroom. It is time to forget that now
and report on my own inner life. I can only say that it feels
as if I have a song in my soul.

Amid the monstrosities of tourism that besmirch this
island, there's an ecumenical Catholic church with its own
evocative symbolism for the Week of Prayer for Christian
Unity. Clusters of iron on the outside resemble the broken
pipes of an organ, the dissonance of a divided church. The
church attracts Christians from many traditions and varied
nationalities. Particularly striking is the stained glass of the
west window through which light penetrates at various
angles. Christ is the Light at the center, calling me to reso-
nance and wholeness. The elegance of this church is at vari-

ance with the tawdry displays of tourism that envelop it. It's
a scenario replicated around the island's circumference. Yet
the heart of the island is another world of mountains, natural forests, and unspoiled villages that could so easily be
overlooked. Isn't it the same with people? It's so easy to judge
a person, as it is a place, at a superficial level. Once one journeys into the heart of a person, the more one discovers. And
this is especially true of spiritual pilgrims, I suppose. Only by
daring to journey inwards can we come close to our real
selves and to God.

This isn't a retreat in the customary sense but an opportunity to be alone with God in a foreign clime. As St. John of
the Cross says: "My Beloved is...strange islands."[15] Once
one's familiar trappings disappear, the masks too are more
easily discarded. While walking across a long stretch of
beach yesterday, I sensed there were two of us by the water's
edge. I think it's always seemed that way. The more alone one
is, the nearer Christ is. Inevitably what seems like a miracu-
lous escape encourages a reexamination of priorities. This
convalescence has helped crystallize so much of what has
been simmering in me and, as the retreat draws to a close, I
believe I can start to clarify what I really feel God wants of
me on this pilgrimage of faith.

I am braced for the next stage.

2

RETRACING STEPS

Move not, speak not—look to the pillar of the
cloud. See how it moves, then follow.
CARDINAL JOHN HENRY NEWMAN

I am sitting in a Parisian café named after my guardian
angel, St. Michael. It takes its title from the bridge
across the road. I'm studying it carefully because a priest
friend recently told me not to think of myself as being spiritually on a bridge but actually *as* the bridge. I like the definition of a priest as *pontifex,* or bridge-builder. Over a toasted
croissant, I look out through the window and watch the
police blowing whistles to tell pedestrians it is safe to cross.
Sirens occasionally pierce the spring air. It strikes me that so
much life goes on around and across the bridge that the stone
viaduct itself is barely noticeable. That's the thing about
bridges, I guess. They don't necessarily stand out. Bridges
allow us to reach places we wouldn't otherwise connect with.
Some bridges are impressively constructed; others are less
grand, taken for granted or simply walked over, walked on,
walked across. Bridges take the weight—they have to be
strong, even though their might is hidden. Here, traffic
moves swiftly over the Seine, while people hurry across. But
not all of them. I see a woman on crutches struggling to get
over and a woman standing with a box in aid of the Society
of St. Vincent de Paul.

I recollect some words of the French orthodox theologian Paul Evdokimov, regarded as a bridge between East and West. He says that in the immense cathedral which is the Universe of God, each person, whether scholar or manual laborer, is called to act as the priest of his whole life—to take all that is human, and to turn it into an offering and a hymn of glory. This encapsulates all I feel about the uniqueness of vocation.

Perhaps, as a journalist, reporting both sides of the argument, I have been something of a bridge-builder. But I've also had "the crippling capacity to see both sides of the same question," as the former archbishop of Canterbury Robert Runcie once described his own difficulties in taking a stance. This may account for my "both-and" psychology.

Today I am retracing my spiritual journey to the church in which I was baptized, at a marble font graced by statues of the twelve apostles. Even though the parish came under the auspices of the Church of England, I didn't hear anyone using the word "Anglican" to describe its identity. The priest always talked about "the Catholic faith" and explained that, at Holy Communion, we received the Blessed Sacrament— the Body and Blood of Christ. There were celebrations of the Eucharist every day of the week. I served at the high altar on Sundays and on other days in the Lady Chapel, where the consecrated hosts were reserved and before which I would instinctively genuflect. I lived an adolescence rooted in the celebration of the Mass when the priest stood with his back to the people. One of my most powerful memories is of serving at the annual Eucharist for the Feast of the Assumption, which was held in the ruins of a local Benedictine abbey. One August the heavens opened and we all had to huddle around the crypt altar as the torrent hemmed us in. It was one of the most atmospheric Masses I have ever experienced. "I feel such an affinity with you, Michael," said Father John on one occasion, when we were walking back to the neighboring retreat house. And on another, one morning after I had been serving in the Lady Chapel, he asked if I were aware of any signs that God might be calling me to be a priest. I was seventeen at the time and was completely taken aback. I had to absorb the implications of his words for a second or two, then answered with a definitive "No." I really didn't feel priesthood in my bones, as many seminarians do.

Almost the only (but, of course, significant) difference between our church's form of Catholicism and the Roman Catholic variety was that there was no mention of the pope. But then nobody referred to the archbishop of Canterbury either, and the queen was acknowledged only as part of the traditional prayers for the realm. It was a sincere living-out of an authentic spiritual life, evolving from a sacramental understanding of the Church and a social gospel among the sick and the homeless. I was encouraged to preach on a regular basis and lead services, invitations which rarely, if ever, come the way of lay people in the Roman Catholic Church.

However, after the much-loved Father John retired, I gradually became disillusioned with the Church of England and felt increasingly marginalized as a Catholic within it. Across the country, the sense of the sacred seemed to be fading as new rites of worship were ushered in—in much the same way, I would later discover, as Vatican II liturgies were alarming some Roman Catholics. It was a disheartening phase for someone who hadn't flown far from the nest, and was compounded by an innate restlessness.

Around this time I happened to become friends with some Roman Catholics my own age and bonded with them naturally. In those pre-university days, their friendship seemed to provide me with an opportunity for spiritual growth and intellectual maturity. After a period of instruction, I was eventually received into the Catholic Church on the memorial of St. Martin of Tours. St. Martin (316–397) had been a soldier in the Roman army until his conversion and baptism. Before becoming a bishop, he helped found the first monastery in Gaul. It was an appropriate date because I

have since felt more at home in monastic settings (Catholic or
Anglican) than in parish congregations. I like the account by
Sulpicius Severus who points out that, despite fulfilling episcopal duties, St. Martin never forsook his original purpose of
living the holy life of a monk. At one time he used a cell next
door to the church, but "because of the unendurable turmoil
of those who came in crowds to him there, he set himself up
in a monastery two miles out of the city, at a spot so hidden
and retired as to suit a hermit's solitude."[16] He was an ideal
spiritual mascot to herald the new path I had chosen.

But instead of feeling I was "home at last," as the spirit of
the reception rite suggested, I felt completely displaced. Indeed,
during the week before the ceremony, I had felt some reluctance
to go forward. Perhaps other people's expectations had spurred
me on—just as they might have once persuaded me to consider
Anglican ordination. Loyal friends from the Anglican parish
turned up at the back of the church that evening. I loved them
so much and felt torn when I saw them there. Far from being
an occasion for celebration, I felt I was being sentenced for life.
The psychological and the spiritual within me were locked in
battle. Nostalgia and imagination were on a collision course. I
wanted this new life—but I wanted the old one as well. I had
always been a Catholic and believed the same theological
truths. At a small party after the reception, a Roman Catholic
friend gave me a card congratulating me on my "First Holy
Communion." I kissed her, but inwardly I was mortified: I had
received the Blessed Sacrament for the first time twelve years
before and wasn't prepared to denigrate the past. I didn't like
the word "convert" either: I knew one could only convert to
another religion—and I had neither renounced my Christianity
nor disowned my Anglicanism. I declined to be confirmed again
because I felt secure in the rite bestowed on me as a teenager in
my home church.

In the months that followed, reverse thrust set in. I
started to resent the new institution and would become so
incensed by some of its rulings that I could not bring myself

to go to communion. At the same time I wondered if I had betrayed my roots. It was the exclusive nature of Roman Catholicism that particularly angered me. My family couldn't come to church with me and receive the sacrament. I realized this during my instruction, of course, but I had grown up in a tradition where any communicant member of another denomination could receive at the Lord's altar, and I wanted such hospitality transferred. After all, the Last Supper was celebrated among Jews, not Roman Catholics or Anglicans. I started to oscillate between the two traditions and was particularly hurt when a Roman Catholic said to me one day: "Our turn is it, this week?" I was caught between worlds and did not find much sympathy for my dilemma in either. Furthermore, a Roman Catholic from the new church asked me if I would try to reconvert a dying Anglican in my old parish because she believed he had been born a Roman Catholic! I felt called to a denomination that did not exist, but all people appeared to care about was which side I was on and to which mast I was going to nail my colors. It seemed I was at the center of a soul-baiting contest. Had we really moved on from the sixteenth century?

My strict media formation within the cloisters of objectivity enabled me to appreciate the doctrines of both traditions, yet I remained convinced my "Anglican" upbringing had been Catholic. But it was in my role as a reporter that my new religious affiliation met with the most suspicion, especially when new contacts in the Catholic parish yielded stories for the newspaper. And once, while covering a news event, I was verbally accosted by two evangelicals from the local Christian bookstore shouting publicly: "Papist! Traitor!" Certainly switching traditions in your own town, especially when you're a religious correspondent, is a dangerous move.

I wanted dual citizenship and felt like the son of divorced parents, trying to bring them back together again. But, over the years, I came to accept that the undeniable pain

and frustration were, in fact, enriching my spirituality. I
learned to worship the God who was beyond denominations
and came to understand in the wilderness so much about
trust, love, and freedom. Some people initially wondered
whether I had raced into Roman Catholicism as a means of
evading my true vocation to be an Anglican priest. I didn't
think so. But I wasn't certain. Perhaps my "priestly" vocation was to be a bridge between the two traditions. This was
really the sort of ecumenical priest I wanted to be. Indeed,
whenever I imagined myself as a priest, it was never as someone running a parish, but as a fellow pilgrim at the bedside
of a dying person on a journey between two lives. I have
always been drawn to the borderline where I can imbibe the
air of paradox. While I was recovering at home from the car
crash, an Anglican priest brought with him a host from the
tabernacle of a Roman Catholic retreat house where he happened to be staying. The nuns had given him permission.
That's the kind of pre-Reformation Christian I am.

I identify with the work of Brother David Steindl-Rast
who says that, as a Benedictine monk, he stands "in the
Christian tradition, its catholic form, which I would spell
with a small *c. Catholic* means 'all-embracing.' I believe in
the human heart. I believe in Common Sense (capital *C*, capital *S*), which is the deepest insight we have in the depths of
our hearts and is common to all of us."[17] I like Steindl-Rast's
description of Catholicism as "all-embracing" but the institution does not always live up to that definition.

I have discovered a wonderful quotation from Thomas
Merton in a book by Ron Sietz, *A Song for Nobody:*

> But you must know one thing, Ron—and it's most
> important. The true church is not that institution,
> not that hierarchy, not that formal organization
> which so hurt you as a child and which is now the
> target of your rage....The true church is a living
> community of love! Now you take what you want

and what you need and what is good from that
other so-called 'church' and then you go on and
live your life in joy.

Merton was courageous for his time. But, as Archbishop
Rowan Williams has noted, both Merton and Bede Griffiths,
the Benedictine monk who lived in an ashram in South India,
spoke from the desert because they—in a sense—made themselves homeless by putting themselves on the edge of the life
of the conventional church and its habits: "Both started out
as safe Catholic converts and good monks; as they went on,
they became rather more shaky Catholics in the eyes of many
and very unusual monks. They became familiar with a desert
landscape in which the external points of orientation were
elusive; they had to find another kind of map."[18]

I am also inspired, here in France, by a book from the
pen of Pierre Solignac who writes that Christians must identify themselves, not with institutional burdens, but with Jesus
Christ who shifted the center of gravity in religion and redefined the way that leads to God. Christ was "the very type of
the free man, challenging all the structures of his time."[19] I
identify with Solignac's point about autonomy.

But is it really possible to emulate that kind of Christ in
today's Church?

3

DANCE OF THE SANDPIPERS

O God, enlarge within us the sense of fellow-ship with all living things.

ST. BASIL THE GREAT

I'm ambling along a stretch of beach in San Francisco, beside the pounding Pacific. As I make tracks in the wet sand, I catch sight of hundreds of sandpipers orchestrating their own dance as they run and fly in and out of the water. In the setting sun, it is a majestic choreography. One member of the troupe has only one leg but can still pull off a pirouette in front of an approaching wave. The little white birds then congregate on the shoreline, like actors grouping to discuss their matinee performance. As they unite, they form a community of grace. Each makes its own contribution to the dance, but together they create harmony and wonder on the coastline. As I stand and watch, I am reminded that it is our uniqueness that counts. God creates out of diversity not uniformity. These creatures reassure me that vocation is about freedom, not conformity.

Birds hold their own place of honor in the Christian spiritual tradition, mirroring the divine life through their extraordinary beauty and fragility. The twelfth-century Victorine mystic Richard of St. Victor even likens the contemplation of God—the highest form of knowledge—to birds hovering in the air. In *The Mystical Ark,* he writes:

"One may see others suspending themselves in one and the same place for a long time with trembling and often rapidly vibrating wings and, through motion, maintain themselves motionless by their agitation (contemplation)."[20]

Although God's pursuit of us has been likened to a "hound of heaven," my experience of vocation is much gentler. The Holy Spirit waits in the wings. Una Kroll, a family doctor who became an Anglican priest, believes the Holy Spirit is sometimes reluctant to cross boundaries and tends to linger in border country. He never forces entry but asks for our cooperation. Una Kroll writes:

> The Holy Spirit who can transcend all boundaries, who can enter where and when He will, is gracious in waiting until He is invited to come and be present with us through baptism. The Holy Spirit is equally gracious in waiting to become present in the Eucharist so that the offered elements of bread and wine become for us the Body and Blood of Christ.[21]

God gives us our space and does not encroach, according to the orthodox writer Metropolitan Anthony, who was Exarch of the Russian Orthodox Church in Western Europe; he thinks that, while the world demands our attention, God entreats us diffidently. The outside world asserts itself. The world within can be sensed but never clamors for attention. Metropolitan Anthony suggests we should look out for the inner world like a bird-watcher who takes up his position in the woods or the fields that are silent, yet vibrating with life. This attentiveness allows us to perceive what might otherwise escape our awareness. Another way of putting it would be to say that it allows us to detect the extraordinary in the ordinary.

Metropolitan Anthony recalls what an old monk once said to him: "The Holy Spirit is like a great shy bird which has alighted a little way off. When you see It coming closer, don't move, don't frighten It, let It come up to you." The story, he suggests, may make us think of the descent of the Holy Spirit in the shape of a dove: "This image of a bird flying down and, at the same time, ready to give itself, is scriptural and full of meaning."[22]

In our search to find our true vocation, these descriptions might make us reconsider our perceptions of God. I cannot relate to a Creator who coerces or manipulates. Gentleness is the divine hallmark. This quality manifests itself in the legends associated with St. Francis, whose love of creation exemplifies the Christian approach to stewardship and compassion. The accounts also speak of the diversity and tenderness of vocation. There are as many ways of serving God as there are birds. Each is different...

Once, when Francis and another friar are walking in the Venetian marshes, they come upon a huge flock of birds, singing among the reeds. The saint remarks to his companion, "Our sisters the birds are praising their Creator. We will go in among them and sing God's praise, chanting the divine office." The birds remain where they are, making so much noise that the friars are unable to hear themselves saying the office. Eventually Francis turns to them and says, "My sisters, stop singing until we have given God the praise to which he has a right." The birds fall silent, remaining that way until Francis gives them permission to sing again, after the brothers have sung their own praises.[23]

According to *The Little Flowers*, when Francis reaches Savurniano, he bids the twittering swallows to keep silence until he has finished preaching. The birds obey. All the men and women of the town are so inspired by his words that Francis decides to institute the Third Order "for the universal salvation of all men." He proceeds on his journey between Cannaio and Bevagno. Full of fervor, he lifts his eyes and notices certain trees close to the road and upon them "an almost infinite number of birds." Marveling at the sight, he turns to his companions and says: "You shall await me here on the road, and I will go and preach to the birds, my sisters." He walks into the field and begins to preach to the birds on the ground, who are soon joined by those in the trees. All stand still until he has finished preaching. St. Francis then goes about among them, touching them with his mantle. None move—and do not depart until Francis has given them a blessing. According to the hagiographer, St. Francis preaches after this manner:

> My sisters the birds, you are much obliged to God your creator, and always and in every place you ought to praise Him, because He has given you liberty to fly wherever you will and has clothed you with twofold and threefold raiment. Moreover, He preserved your seed in Noah's Ark that your race might not be destroyed. Again, you are obliged to Him for the element of the air which He has appointed for you. Furthermore, you sow not, neither do you reap, yet God feeds you and gives you rivers and fountains from which to drink. He gives you mountains and valleys for your refuge, and high trees in which to build your nests. And, since you know neither how to sew or to spin, God clothes you and your little ones; so, clearly your Creator loves you, seeing that He gives you so many benefits. Guard yourselves, therefore, you sisters the birds, from the sin of ingratitude and be ever mindful to give praise to God.

As St. Francis speaks these words, all the birds began to open their beaks, stretch their necks, expand their wings, and reverently bow their heads to the ground. By these motions and their songs, they demonstrate that the saint has given them "very great delight." Francis rejoices with them, marveling at so great a multitude of birds and at their most beautiful diversity as well as their attentiveness and fearlessness, "for which he devoutly praises the Creator in them." St. Francis makes the sign of the cross and gives them leave to depart. They rise into the air "with wondrous songs" and, according to the form of the cross with which St. Francis has blessed them, they separate into four bands and fly east, west, south, and north to the four corners of the earth. Each company sings marvelous songs, echoing the preaching of the cross of Christ about to be spread throughout the world by Francis and his friars. The friars, like the birds, "possess nothing of their own in this world but commit their lives wholly to the providence of God."[24]

As I write this, I think of the stories my grandfather used to tell me in front of a log fire. Only now do I realize how integral they were to my spiritual development. When he was working on a large country estate, he got to know a pair of robins who nested in a crevice. They did everything together. One morning he discovered that the hen had been killed by a vole-trap, even though it had been tunneled off to keep the birds out. After that, the cock didn't appear for several weeks but, one day, suddenly turned up again—minus an eye and a set of toes. He had obviously been hit by the trap as well but had managed to escape. For the next six years the disabled robin became my grandfather's close companion. Every time he made a distinct sound with his lips, the robin would appear, perch on his hand, and eat cheese, bread-crumbs, and cake. He seemed frightened of everyone else.

If my grandfather walked to the greenhouses, his red-breasted pal would come too, waiting patiently outside until the jobs had been completed. Then he would follow him around again, even flying beside my grandfather's bicycle as he rode home from work at meal times. Despite his handi-caps, the robin managed to rear several families and was always protective. He would take food from my grandfa-ther's hand and fly back to the rock plant crevices where the nests had been built. Every night for years, my grandfather would shut the robin in the orangery to roost on the trees and let him out again the following morning. But one evening, he forgot to put him inside, and they never met again. Although my grandfather related the tale in the context of the wild, it holds a spiritual significance; it teaches an attitude toward the most vulnerable in society and the need to own our own vulnerability in the process of becoming ourselves. Moreover, it symbolizes the relationship between a gentle God and his beloved creation, no matter our disability, inadequacy, or fragility.

The secrets of our vocation are embedded in the natural world.

4

RISK AND DISCOVERY

*One does not discover new lands without
consenting to lose sight of the shore.*

ANDRÉ GIDE

On my first assignment to New York, I'm learning
about different forms of vocation. I feel so at home
reporting here. Why do I want to become an ordained priest
when I have the world as my parish? Journalism is a passport
into other people's lives.

I hail a yellow cab, adorned with flowers. As I make my
escape from the deafening streets, I am surprised to hear the
peaceful chords of J. S. Bach "to beat the boredom and beat
the traffic." I like the incongruity. The taxi driver, who is
black, tells me how a white policeman beat him and locked
him up following some confusion between his cab and some
police cars. "He started to call me names, took my license,
and then he threw it on the ground. I went down to pick it
up and he ran the car almost over me. I ran in the car. He
then beat me up and locked me out. I made a complaint but
it was one cab driver against four police officers." I believe
his story and persuade him to put it on tape for the five-part
documentary I am here in the Big Apple to make.

I go on to the 44th Precinct police station in the Bronx
to record interviews about drug-related homicide. It's a
dilapidated, "Old West" style building off the highway. An

32

armed guard stands by the entrance. Inside I meet an officer with guns strapped to his waist. He tells me about the courage it takes to be a cop in this city. "I was doing a midnight [shift]," he says. "We were on routine patrol and we encountered a group of men with guns. It was a scary moment. As we faced them, we didn't know exactly what we had until it was all over and we found the semiautomatic weapons. It could have gone either way. The only people we are a threat to are the criminal element. They see us as the enemy. There are a lot of good hardworking people here and it's up to us to prevent crime from spreading. If God's on our side, we will do so." The officer tells me a strong religious commitment underpins his work. "I see people as they are. I don't try to judge them. What I try to do is look into what they are all about, especially when I deal with kids. I see how they were brought up. I ask them questions and most of the time you see that, when kids turn bad, it's because they lack a parent." My calling is to convey these stories sensitively and fairly, acting as a bridge perhaps between the communities.

Today I make my way down to Wall Street in Lower Manhattan. The New York Stock Exchange is closed but within its shadow a refuge for the city's marginalized people has its doors wide open—Trinity Church. Trinity has invested its shares in a program for the victims of social injustice. I attend the Saturday morning Eucharist there. It is celebrated by the vicar, the Rev. Canon Lloyd Casson, a black priest. As I watch him at the altar, I start to envisage myself there. I like the ethos of this place. It's my kind of church. It's doing theology on the edge. After the service, Father Lloyd tells me that Trinity actually predates the United States. It was chartered by King William in the 1690s to be the Anglican church for the colony of New York, so it operates with an authority predating the nation. "There have been three buildings but we have never moved from this site," he tells me.

I decide to disclose why I am visiting New York. Father Lloyd agrees to go on the record. I have my questions lined up but know that, at another level, I am testing my own vocation through the interview. I learn that Trinity is identified, not only as a house of worship, but also as a community that "cares deeply" about what happens in the city of New York. It has greeted waves of immigrants, not only by setting up schools, but also by making it possible for people to learn English and assimilate into American society and to receive medical care and social-welfare benefits. The more Father Lloyd talks, the more I want to be his curate. He explains that Trinity has even helped South Bronx Churches, an ecumenical organization with a million-dollar revolving loan to build houses for low-income people in the community. There's also a drop-in center in lower Manhattan for homeless people, as well as a shelter in St. Paul's Chapel where George Washington said his prayers after his inauguration.

"What makes our work dangerous is that we don't turn anyone away," says Father Lloyd. "We are open to whoever comes and try to be helpful in terms of small material assistance or referrals. All day long there are people who would be considered by some other places undesirable. We do not turn anyone away. Some have been deinstitutionalized from psychiatric hospitals and other places. They are people whose situation has driven them, frankly, out of their minds. We often bear the brunt of their anger, fear, and hurt."

With my application for the ordained ministry being processed back in England, I am fascinated to find out why Lloyd Casson decided to become a priest. He tells me he was born in Wilmington, Delaware. His was a poor community dubbed by others as "a slum" or "a ghetto." As a youngster, he had to learn how to defend himself and reckons such instincts still assist him in his ministry. "At least it makes it possible for me not to be initially afraid of people in trouble," he points out. "Wilmington was a segregated town in those days but one in which education was a premium. I feel good about the fact that my family, extended family, and teachers insisted that all of us should be educated so we could make a significant contribution to our society. Today there's a resurgence of racism in New York as there is in this country. We still have the tendency, even in the church at large, to make many judgments about people in terms of race. But we have a great start here as Trinity demonstrates what God's will is for all God's people—to be one. Surely the Lord's table ought to be the place where we can all gather?"

Lloyd Casson thinks his very vulnerability as a black priest enables him to be a more sensitive minister. He gradually cultivated an awareness of the way people treat and victimize him because of his race. He has known what it means to seek acceptance. He feels called to be, not only a strong and active fighter for social justice and civil rights, but also a reconciler. He has been wounded in many ways so he too can heal wounds. He says he can spot them as well. "I think that, as far as people are concerned, the beginning of a relationship is recognizing that there's something you share in common. One of the things I have in common with other people in this world is hurts. I can see the hurts in people I reach out to and touch. I also experience *their* touch."

New York is a city filled with pain but also with tremendous potential, he believes, for people of all cultures and backgrounds to share their talents for the creation of a society in which all can have a stake, an opportunity, and a share. "For me that is at the heart of the Gospel. That's what I think I'm called to do. I think that is what is beginning to happen at Trinity and, if we can make it happen here, I believe that we can help to be an instrument of healing for the rest of our city.

After talking to Lloyd Casson, I feel I *would* like to be a priest—but only in his mold. Yet I have to keep asking myself whether I am really being *called* by God into this particular ministry.

Even though much has happened, I haven't written in this journal for many months. Unbelievably, a few weeks ago (a year after the last accident), another drunk driver crashed into my car as I was heading into work to read the first radio news bulletin of the day. My car veered off the road, and the inebriated woman carried on meandering down the motorway. As I stood waiting for the police, I felt I must have been saved again for a reason. Since I last wrote in this journal, I was selected to train as a non-stipendiary priest so I could combine my journalism with my ministerial preparation. But the irregular work shifts and the inflexible nature of the course conspired against me. I managed to keep the plates spinning for a term but this was no way to train for the sacred ministry. More significantly, I didn't have the deep sense of inner certainty that other candidates for ordination seemed to have. Some officials in the church don't easily mask their suspicion (or envy) of someone who wants to live in both worlds. It's all to do with perceptions of power and freedom. It makes me wonder about those who become ordained for reasons of self-aggrandizement. I feel much more at home in situations of powerlessness. That's where I feel closest to God. The sense of being called is still strong but its meaning remains opaque. At some point I think I will have to test whether or not I am being called to be a full-time parish priest, even though there is strong resistance to this on my part. It does not seem *me*, even though I am strongly drawn to the pastoral and spiritual dimensions of the work. I would like to be alongside the sick. I would like to comfort the bereaved. But I don't want to be a figurehead in the community.

I'm meditating this morning on the Gospel words: "If any want to become my followers, let them deny themselves and take up their cross daily and follow me" (Luke 9:23). Christ doesn't impose himself on me but keeps the invitation open. It's clear from these words that the initiative to be drawn out needs to be centered on God and not me. The very following may involve darkness, fog, conflict, but any journey of faith will also reveal new horizons. A journey that precludes risk or self-denial isn't a journey at all because to travel means to move out and away from the familiar.

Only then can we discover the depths within.

5

ARTISTS OF THE ETERNAL

Acquire inward peace, and thousands around
you will find their salvation.

ST. SERAPHIM OF SAVOV

Time and again I return to an article by the Irish writer John O'Donohue. In "The Priestliness of the Human Heart," O'Donohue sees priestliness as a participation in the creative and transfigurative nature of God. The call to priestliness is a voice whispering at the ontological heart of every life. Priestliness is ontological. Only in a secondary sense can it be considered functional; even then, in explicit priesthood, its function is to awaken and realize the implicit priestliness of each person. The call to explicit priesthood comes out of the recognition of this deeper implicit priestliness. Priesthood longs to awaken the *who* to its origin, presence, possibility, and promise. In this way priesthood attempts to awaken the fecundity of being to the possibilities of its own becoming. Consequently, priesthood is ministry to the deepest nature and identity of the person. A vocation to the priesthood is "a calling to the realization of one's priestliness in the service of the implicit priestliness of all people. This vocation is akin to the vocation of an artist....The artist is called to minister to the eternal, to bring its unseen forms to visibility....A priest is an artist of the eternal." I warm to this imagery.

I am woken up this morning by the sound of desperate scratching and fluttering in the kitchen flue. I can't reach the bird trapped inside, so call the fire service, which arrives in a blaze of red, confusing puzzled neighbors who haven't detected any smoke. Spreading their helmets on the pine table, they drill out a panel and discover a frightened starling struggling for air. The bird soon flies through the open window to freedom. It reminds me of a line from one of the psalms: "Like birds, our souls flew away." The divine light brings us freedom "to live a life of love," as the Second Letter of John puts it. If we are cut off from God, through our own darkness, we cannot live the life God desires of us. For me, the trapped starling becomes an image of my being imprisoned in a cassock and collar, unable to escape.

"You beheld the trouble of my soul." This psalm seems appropriate today because I want to take shelter in the Lord from the Church! Why do the attitudes of some institutionalized priests make me doubt even more strongly that the ordained ministry is right for me? They appear to come from the head and not from the heart. They remind me of Sartre's story of the waiter who, from self-deception, performs his job too keenly. They seem to be acting out a role, rather than allowing their true inner selves to emerge. This troubles me because the more I encounter the living God, the more I want to understand my true self—and I do not want to play a part. I want to *be*.

My early morning news-reading shifts are monastic in the sense that I arise in the dark. I have to be in the news-room at 5 a.m. to prepare the first bulletin of the day, and it's a half-hour drive to the studios. So I get up at 3:30 a.m. to spend half an hour in prayer to fortify me for a relentless day. I have never been so disciplined. Before going into work today, I reflect on lines from Psalm 62: "My body is pining for your presence....I long to adore you....Your love is better than life....Your right hand is holding me safe." I ask for an awareness of God's holding me safe. I feel peaceful, relaxed, and secure during the meditation by candlelight. The flickering flame symbolizes constant movement and initiative on God's part. The shadow thrusts above the cross, then shimmers forward, pushing out and suggesting new paths. But does this signify *priesthood*? Why does this word have a hold on me? Some of the prayer disintegrates into thinking about friends and situations, perhaps overanalysis, but on the whole I am at one with myself and with God. At one point I get caught up "in the shadow of his wings."

The prayer confirms something about not being able to serve two masters. If I am to be my true self—the Christ self—I have to be single-minded and clear in my vocation. I am increasingly conscious of the impossibility of split loyalties. Much as I love what I do, I have to acknowledge that I do feel sapped and disorientated by the constantly revolving work shifts. Perhaps I am being led toward a new form of journalistic work to make the dual vocation possible? A television program tonight tells the story of hymn writer John Newton ordained at thirty-nine after a life as a sailor. A series of escapes from misfortune led him to believe that he had been saved for some purpose. Interesting...

After writing a sermon on the temptations in the desert, I ruminate on words from Ephesians 3—"filled with all the fullness of God." It is unexpectedly and swiftly actualized in that a great sense of God's love, spirit, and power fills my very being with a peace so overwhelming I wonder if I can remain there. I am reminded of a famous phrase of Rudolf Otto, one of the most influential religious thinkers in the first half of the twentieth century. In *The Idea of the Holy*, Otto describes an experience that, he argues, underlies all religion. He calls it the "numinous." It has three components: *mysterium tremendum et fascinans*. As *mysterium,* the numinous is "wholly other"—entirely different from anything we experience in ordinary life. Our response can be only one of silence. The numinous is also a *mysterium tremendum*. This provokes terror because it is perceived as an overwhelming power. It is also *fascinans*—merciful and gracious. I sense a fusion of all three in what I have just experienced. It's as though the holiness of God is penetrating my very being, right down to the bones in my feet. I need to tell someone or at least to record it. A feeling of being called or singled out for a purpose is evident. Decisions about the future must emerge from the God-Me, deep in my center. Whatever lies afoot, I am assured that God will be there in every situation, in the joy as well as in the conflict. As I become aware of this, I feel I have to channel the power passing through my open hands so I pray for those who are sick. In my frequent dreams about priesthood, I am often being raised up with hands outstretched.

Today is the memorial of St. Augustine who wrote: "Our hearts are restless until they rest in you." It is a timely day to meet and interview Henri Nouwen, whose writings on the spiritual life, not least on restlessness, have inspired me for more than a decade. If there's anyone who should ordain me, it's him! When we eventually meet in Northampton, England, he isn't completely as I had imagined but I know it is him. In terms of appearance, he is tall and thin, and has balding black-

gray hair, glasses, deep eyes, and large hands that spring into
action as soon as he speaks. He wears a blue-checked flat cap,
scarf, and raincoat, and carries a red shoulder bag. He has to
be Dutch! He darts about with great alacrity. As well as an
almost tangible holiness, there is an ordinariness about him,
along with hospitality and warmth. He is intense and passion-
ate: energetic one minute, then quiet, reflective, absorbed the
next. After the interview I drive him to a Christian arts festival. I tell him that I have long planned to do postgraduate
research into his life and spirituality. I ask about sources. I am
surprised when he replies that he doesn't have any. He loves
art. He loves conversations.

The autonomous priest and theologian is booked to give
several talks at the festival, which is being staged in the middle of the countryside. We trek through the mud, holding our
trousers above our ankles and laughing as we slop about in
the mire. Two Franciscans in their brown habits seem color-
coordinated. Nouwen admits he's ambitious, but he commu-
nicates a genuine humility. It seems symbolic to be walking
through the wet humus with him. In the hospitality tent, he
spies a bishop and asks me his name. Then he rushes over to
introduce himself. He invites the bishop to have coffee. The
bishop hesitates. Henri pleads: "Won't you sit down and join
us?" The bishop backs off: "Maybe later. I have to give a talk
in a couple of minutes." Henri looks disappointed, then
spots another speaker. "Who's that?" And he's gone.

Lunch with Henri is a moving experience. He joins
hands with me, giving thanks and praying for the afternoon.
We have zucchini and cucumber soup, a roll, and salad.
Henri shares his small piece of cheese with me because my
meal is the last to be served. It is a eucharistic moment.
Henri's spirituality is one of gratitude. After the meal, he
insists on going to the back of the tent to thank the waitress,
despite pleas from a friend to move toward the arena where
he is due to speak soon on "Being the Beloved." He looks
anxious, wondering what he will say. But once he is in front

of the young audience, his nerves are transformed into a charismatic confidence, his hands and posture reflecting his emotions of the moment. Then he holds his head in silent prayer. Afterwards, he thanks me for staying to listen to him and tells me to keep in touch. He seems sad to say farewell. The occasion stays with me on the journey home and throughout the evening. Something has happened. I feel I have walked with a very holy person and am now inspired to live a more authentic spiritual life.

Listening to the taped interview, I hear Henri say something that hadn't made an impression on me at the time— that, for twenty years or so, he felt his career was his vocation. Then he began to feel that it no longer was. So he had to find out what that might be. He left university life and went to South America. But he didn't sense a vocation there. He returned to academic life. But after a while he still didn't feel called to that world any longer either. Then the L'Arche community in Canada called him to be their pastor. He didn't invite himself. They invited him. I engage with Nouwen's searching. I feel that my existing career may no longer be vocation and that I must move elsewhere. Nouwen's call was to an environment he least expected.

I must be ready for that too.

6

SEARCHING'S BEAUTY

How good and pleasant it is,
when brothers live in unity!
PSALM 133

*I*n August 1940, with Europe in the grip of war, a young Swiss Protestant, Roger Schultz, set up home in the desolate village of Taizé, here in the Burgundy region of France. He wanted to bring together people who would live out what he called "a parable of community." In his house he hid refugees, mostly Jews fleeing the Nazi occupation. Out of his courage and faith grew a unique community that now comprises ninety brothers from over twenty countries, of Catholic and a variety of Protestant backgrounds. I'm staying here for a few days to make a documentary, but it's the perfect place to consider an ecumenical calling.

Yesterday I spent half an hour with Brother Roger and have now woken up in the middle of the night feeling moved by the experience. Three weeks after my meeting with Henri Nouwen, I know I have been in the presence of another holy person, welcomed by knowing blue eyes and a smiling, tanned face lined with years of struggle and contemplation. "It's not necessary to learn to be vulnerable, that's part of human nature," he once remarked. "The wound in every human being…makes us all vulnerable beings. All through my life, especially when I was young, I have sung for hours,

44

until I attained joy and serenity. Sometimes I have to sing soundlessly, so as not to disturb others."

Brother Roger, who thought about becoming a writer before entering the monastic life, says his maternal grand-mother discovered intuitively "a sort of key" to the ecumeni-cal vocation and opened a way for him to put it into practice. Marked by the witness of his grandmother's life and follow-ing her vision, Brother Roger discovered his own Christian identity by "reconciling within myself the faith of my origins with the mystery of the Catholic faith, without breaking fel-lowship with anyone." This personal working-out of faith appeals to me, as does Brother Roger's image of a gentle God. "He never forces our hand," he once said. "God is so careful of human freedom that at times he is so silent that our hearts almost break. God made himself humble so as not to blind us by his overwhelming, infinite beauty, by a love which would overpower us. God gives all and asks nothing in return. That is why, for anyone who chooses the absolute call, there is no happy medium."

I interview the prior in his sparsely furnished room with its orange curtains, matching shades and bedspread, a large round pine table, chairs, stools, books, flowering plants, and a tin of chocolate biscuits. A map of the world is a reminder of the community's international connections and the meet-ings it arranges in European cities as well in America and Asia. At one point Brother Roger, wearing a white linen alb, sits at his desk and writes me a prayer in French, which trans-lates as "Dear Mike, Thanks be to God for all that you are. I will always keep you fresh in my heart." These generous words will bless the onward journey.

I feel rooted in this ecumenical setting and wonder how the thousands of young people who flock here from all cor-ners will be able to live out the spirit of Taizé in their lives back home. "Above all, let them live each day, let them let go of their anxiety if that is possible, and tell them that one day is already a great deal," the prior recommends. There is a

message here for me too. "Let them not be too preoccupied
with the days to come because here is the exceptional situation of the Gospel and the Christian vocation: Christ takes to
his heart of hearts what wounds us, what makes us suffer, or
a trial, and God has already prepared what we shall
become."

During breaks in recording, I take the opportunity to
talk to one of the brothers—he happens to be from the
Reformed tradition—about my oscillation over what I might
become. After listening carefully, he quietly responds by saying I should be grateful for the freedom and opportunities I
have to minister as a layperson. But, as my tale unfolds, he
thinks I should take the question of priesthood seriously.
When he asks me to give an image of myself as a priest, I
instinctively reply: "When I am sitting at the bedside of a suffering person." He says that is "a beautiful image" but adds
that I shouldn't see ministry solely in those terms. There
should be joy in it too.

We arrange to meet for a second time. Without abandoning something, the brother says, I might not be able to
enter something else: "Priesthood is ministry and not some
other kind of work." Then he tells me of a French journalist
who was ordained at the age of fifty-five. Vocation is personal. There might come a day when the desire to be
ordained a priest proves overwhelming. He tells me not to
think too much about it. But if the longing becomes too
strong, I should do it. I will be given back the things I lose. It
is important, however, to wait. It could be wrong to force
myself into work that is not right. "Don't accuse yourself,"
he whispers. "Have the courage to wait until it has become
simple." His words remind me of one those journalistic max-
ims from the training manual—"Make it simple." If only...

If my vocation is to the sacramental priesthood, I will
know, the brother says. Oscillation is a sign of complication.
Priesthood requires renunciation. I need to be free in order to
give freely. "Give thanks for what has been given today and

the work you do. Find joy in that. God has not abandoned you. He has carried you."

Another brother—a Roman Catholic—explains in a recorded interview that the vocation of Christians is "something so beautiful, so important, so vital." Christians cannot escape their vocation. But it's not necessarily a once-and-for-all call. It's a continual beckoning. Although I am taping his words for the broadcast, I allow them to speak to me personally:

> You have to discern which is God's voice and which is your voice. I am one of the brothers who stay every night in the church here to talk with people. They often come with the question: "How can I discern the voice of God?" We have no answer. We cannot say this is God's voice or this is not God's voice. But we try to help them in their discernment, not by giving lots of advice because we are not spiritual masters, but by being people who simply accompany them on their own search. In prayer, they can come to discern, perhaps, where they will be most close to Christ and closest to themselves. This is probably where God's will awaits them. We often find that people discover a call to be close to people in suffering in their own countries, to bring an answer to situations of conflict, and to try to be bearers of reconciliation and trust, often in very humble ways.

You cannot force light on the question of vocation, the brother points out. It takes time. And time is not an enemy but a friend. People have to learn how to wait and to search. They need to see the beauty of searching and not be anguished by the fact that they don't have all the answers. If it is a promise of Christ, they will find it—"Ask, and it will be given you; search, and you will find; knock, and the door will be opened for you."

But how will they know when they have found it? Sometimes people don't realize right away that they have discovered what they were looking for, the brother replies. Vocation starts to crystallize only when they look back on their lives and pose the question: "What made me set out in a certain direction? What made me decide to take a year off, to pray in a community, or to get involved in a project?" It's often only by looking back that they realize it must have been God guiding them. They didn't hear a voice. They didn't hear anyone speaking to them. But it must have been God, they conclude.

So can vocation only be discovered retrospectively? He answers: "I don't know if it's only that but it's sometimes that 'God must have been there if my life took such a direction.' Maybe that was the case for Abraham who set out without knowing where he was going, according to the Letter to the Hebrews. He realized only afterwards that it must have been God speaking to him."

What impresses me about this religious community, as with others I have visited, is that I am among faithful brethren who have responded to a call and made a commitment. I hold the microphone steadily and listen intently as a gently spoken, peaceful young man tells me, in the warm afternoon sunshine, how he followed God's call and became a member of the community. A New Yorker of Puerto Rican origin, Brother Hector grew up in a deprived area of Brooklyn. His family settled in an African-American–Hispanic neighborhood of New York where he experienced his local Catholic church as a place of hope. It was an inner-city ghetto characterized by poverty, violence, and human abandonment. "The church was a sign of life, and it gave a message of life to us especially because the priest and the sisters were very present among the problems of our neighborhood," he explains. "That's where the seeds of my vocation lie." After he came to Taizé, he began to understand that this was true, not only for a tiny parish in Brooklyn, but for the entire Church—God's family on this earth:

> Our first calling is to be people of the Gospel, to live out the Gospel, to seek reconciliation, to try to be people of trust, and to live after the manner of Christ who, when insulted, persecuted, or rejected, never responded with insult or violence. Christ was not frightened to show his anger when the heart of the Gospel was at risk. But it was never for personal reasons. Christ always had a larger vision—to show who God his Father was. At times in the Gospels we can see a Christ who is angry. But this is because the heart of the Gospel is at risk, his mission was at risk, and the reason he has come is also at risk. He wants to complete his mission— what he has come for.

In New York, Brother Hector tries to be "a presence among the poor" in the Hell's Kitchen district. His ministry includes visiting seafarers on board ships, running a center for human rights, caring for the elderly and those who are "shut in and lonely," and creating a community garden, a "space with flowers in the midst of a neighborhood that does not have a lot of beauty sometimes." He tells me:

> When you look at the Gospel, you see that Christ comes to be present to, and to be available for, every single human being without exception. We, too, with the little that we have, and the little that we have understood, even about the Gospel, can be present to others. We too can be Christ for others. We don't have to do that by going out and imposing ourselves on them. By being a presence of kindness, patience, mercy, and compassion, we

can be a presence of Christ for others in the midst
of very difficult situations.

Being the presence of Christ for others strikes me as
being much more fundamental to the notion of vocation than
being caught up in an ecclesiastical system. Some people
seem to regard priesthood as a career, lured by forms of spiritual power. My working retreat at Taizé confirms that, were
I to become a priest, I should want to do so quietly and
remain on the borders of the church.

It is literally an *eccentric* calling—moving out from the
center.

PART TWO
Deep Caverns

7

MOUNTAIN PATHS

God has created me out of love, and my salvation is found in my living out a return of that love. All my choices, then, must be consistent with this given direction in my life.

ST. IGNATIUS LOYOLA

As I was reading a biography of Albert Schweitzer today, some words of his sprang out of the pages as though they were speaking directly to me: "Progress always consists in taking one or other of two alternatives, in abandoning the attempt to combine them." After a successful period as a philosopher, theologian, musician, preacher, and lecturer, Schweitzer journeyed to Africa to build and run a hospital for local people. He had to make considerable sacrifices but was eventually able to integrate, to some extent, his medical gifts with his other talents. As the biographer puts it: "Africa for Schweitzer was not an escape from life, nor the goal of his life. It was the symbol of his life. The meaning was reverence for life." Will the ordained ministry become the symbol of my life? Since I abandoned the idea of priesthood and journalism as a dual calling, I have felt less pressurized. Perhaps Schweitzer is right: Only through making a choice can one progress. But how can we trust it is the right choice?

"For this reason the Father loves me, because I lay down my life in order to take it up again" (John 10:17). During a meditation on darkness, the garbage collectors arrive outside the house to take the rubbish away. This is what I ask of God: Empty me out so I can follow Christ more authentically. Discipleship clearly involves freely handing over in order to reclaim again. Like the Eucharist, we are taken, blessed, broken, and given.

News of the death of an actress I interviewed during my newspaper days fills me with sadness. I imagine her "riddled with cancer" in a wheelchair in a nursing home. Then I look up the profile I wrote of her some years ago; she had said that she hoped to be an actress "into great old age" if her mind and body allowed. They didn't. I feel sad. I want to be with the sick, loving them to the end.

I am back in the Canaries, above the clouds, in a volcanic desert on Tenerife. At a height of 3,718 meters, the summit of *El Teide* is the highest point, not just of the Canary Islands, but of the entire Iberian Peninsula. The ascent through the foothills takes in an abundance of flora and fauna. At about 2,000 meters the vegetation starts to give way to the characteristic lava landscape. It is even possible (with a permit) to venture to the very mouth of *El Teide* and inhale the sulfuric fumes that prove there is still activity deep within this ancient but dormant volcano. An azure sky arches over me like the inside of a large cathedral dome. Around me are millions of burnt stones, once flowing coals, and clumps of icy snow, glistening in the midday sun. In this crater I feel as though I am in someone's soul. There are clusters of shrub and slithering lizards but of course no birds, whose song I miss. Occasionally the voices of explorers can be heard, along with a guide's whistle as two climbers stray dangerously close to the rim. Living on the edge is always risky. I feel extraordinarily close to God up here. I can't resist opening my arms and saying the Our Father out loud. I can understand why Jesus prayed in such landscapes and I remember the words of St. John of the Cross: "My Beloved the Mountains."

As I climb down, I start to see and hear birds again. They look like small swallows. I feel at home among them. I head for a little white chapel I noticed on the way up. I need to go in there. It's locked but I learn that the keys are kept in the local hostel. I hand over my wallet as a surety—they really want my passport but I don't have it with me. In the church I kneel in silence, then prostrate myself before an altar of flowers and a crucifix. I ask God to take my life and make it his. It is an act of handing over. I then place on the altar the gold ring I'd been wearing and ask God's blessing on it. I hear the wind blowing outside. The chapel door opens and bangs. All of a sudden, I no longer feel alone. I glance round anxiously. It's only the wind. Then I realize that, from now on, I must not look back but keep my eyes focused firmly on Christ. I place the ring on the third finger of my right hand as an outward symbol of an inner trust. I offer a prayer of thanksgiving and repentance in front of the altar, repeat the Lord's Prayer, and offer a blessing. I am now sitting at the back of the chapel feeling deeply peaceful and hopeful.

I think this is about priesthood but part of me wonders if I am feeling psychologically and spiritually obliged to test my vocation further.

Four months on, and I am on the other side of the world in Australia. I am reporting on Sydney's Olympic bid, my last news assignment for the BBC. After much thought, I have decided to take the plunge and go off to theological college full-time. "Bless the Lord who filled my soul with life" was the refrain of the responsorial psalm at the Eucharist in Melbourne Cathedral tonight where, among the worshippers of four men, is a person some might label a beggar. On a day when I've been to Ramsay Street to interview some of the cast of *Neighbors,* it is especially important to embrace him as my neighbor. Only yesterday at a church on the outskirts of Adelaide, we celebrated the Feast of St. Lawrence, commemorating a man who welcomed beggars. Simone Weil writes that God even comes like a beggar. I must deflect my eyes from news angles and focus them on the *anawim,* the little, the forgotten, the oppressed. I must share powerlessness before I can preach about it.

But, with just six weeks to go before setting off for seminary, I am wondering why I now feel so attached to this reporting life. After recording an interview at Raffles Hotel in Singapore, I flew on to Sydney for a helicopter tour of the city and its Olympic sites. I interviewed government officials, Olympic sportsmen and women, two aborigines, and the general manager of the Sydney Opera House. I have enough material for a dozen features. There are some great stories here. But it seems this journalistic life must die soon so that something else can be reborn. Why do I have to hand this over? For several years now I have been producing the news and editing the bulletins, rarely moving beyond the studios. But now I am back reporting again and feel this is what I am made for.

Yesterday it happened: I gave up my staff job and moved into the unknown. I tell my colleagues, during a warm and appreciative farewell, that I had once had a dream in which a news anchor's desk turned into an altar, and another where a studio became a church. So I am about to find out if the dreams have any spiritual foundation. I also refer to our coverage of an IRA bombing and how I wished I had been a chaplain at the scene and not the presenter of the reaction program. I also remark about how, at Taizé last year, I watched two Bosnian brothers putting their arms around each other. At the time this had symbolized my dual vocation. I think I saw the boys change support for each other unthinkingly: one put his arm around the other, and then the other did the same. Perhaps I am merely changing arms for a while but there is no denying that, whether it's journalism or priesthood, it's the connection with people that matters most.

How does it feel to have abandoned everything? Well, there's a sense of freedom to move in the right direction—if indeed it *is* the right direction. Although it was touching to bid farewell to my colleagues, friends I love and respect very much, I didn't feel as emotional as I thought I might. Indeed, although the wine was flowing, there was almost a sobriety about the occasion, and I didn't feel like a wild party afterwards. Strange. The severing I had been fearing became a natural moving on, a sort of death one has been dreading but which actually turns out to be the most natural thing in the world.

…Shortly after writing the above, I went into a kind of bereavement and a sense of *acedia* or spiritual boredom like that experienced by the Desert Fathers. It passed after a couple of days and I felt close to God in prayer.

Three weeks to theological college and I have just returned from a holiday touring Germany, Switzerland, and Italy. We flew to Amsterdam where my traveling companion had his wallet pickpocketed on a tram on the way out and I was robbed of my flight bag containing passport, tickets, crucifix, and Bible on the way back. At the northern Italian resort of Lake Como, encased by mountains, I had been preparing for seminary training by studying the notion of priesthood in Leviticus and Hebrews. I also read *I Heard the Owl Call My Name,* Margaret Craven's elegantly crafted novel about a young Anglican priest, who has not long to live, being sent to an Indian village in the wilds of British Columbia. The text has been recommended by the tutors.

It was a replenishing holiday but, toward the end, I became rather despondent and tense. Since leaving the BBC, I have pined a little for the people I have left behind but rarely for the work, although I sensed a pang or two when I walked out of Lucern railway station in Switzerland and saw a television crew. Returning home today, I found a letter from Henri Nouwen on the mat. He has promised to pray for me as I "journey toward the ordained priesthood."

But will that path bring me wholeness?

8

DARK NIGHT

In wintertime, everything that is lovely withers away. All the leaves, which are the natural crown of the beauty of the trees, fall from the branches and are mingled with earth. The song of the birds is silent, the nightingale flies away, the swallow sleeps, and the dove leaves its nest...

GREGORY OF NYSSA

I am writing this in my room at the seminary. It is supposed to be the beginning of a new chapter in my life. I haven't been here a day and already feel completely displaced. Just before leaving home yesterday, I sat on the top of the stairs and didn't think I could go through with it. I felt depressed but gained reassurance from a reading in *The Joy of the Saints* for September 25 (Jean-Pierre de Caussade). It concerned "the temptation of discouragement," which de Caussade says must be resisted with "all your might." So in the end I packed up the car and drove down here. Instead of using the motorway, I took a circuitous route through small country towns, a sign no doubt of prolonging my freedom. Eventually I arrived, moving into two cold rooms and meeting a friendly fellow inmate who piped: "Daunting, isn't it?"

But today has been absolutely dire. I could not for one moment imagine myself as a priest at the altar, as I did in

New York. Perhaps it's because I'm not in an Anglo-Catholic context. The college chapel doesn't have a tabernacle and I feel that absence intensely. I want to leave and am starting to call friends from the pay phone. I am unable to speak to anyone with any degree of relaxation and am sure it is all a nightmare from which I will soon wake. I cannot see myself surviving this. Henri Nouwen says voluntary displacement can be a mark of discipleship—"Jesus Christ is the displaced Lord in whom God's compassion becomes flesh."[25] These are reassuring words but this is so painful for me. I can't read, pray, think—total *acedia*. I pine for everyone and everything I have abandoned to do this. I am angry that I am like this, but I also feel like escaping—fast.

Three days later and I am surprised still to be here. I'm in a state of bewilderment. God seems absent. My prayer is listless and unfocused. The feelings are ones of dread. I fear they will never be expunged. Admitting this to the kind and sympathetic tutors so early in the course was something of a risk, but I feel a sense of relief for having been open with them. I have thought about going back and developing a career in broadcasting, especially as a student says he was moved by my program on Taizé. At times I have *hated* being confined to this life, albeit temporarily. The constant rain hasn't helped. Talk of combining ministry with broadcasting energizes me—the thought of parish work nauseates me. I really do hope I can settle to this. When I left my job, I never dreamt that all this fluctuation would emerge. As I flick through the pages of my journal, I note that when I have talked about "full-time ministry" I have *never* used the term "parish"! Broadcasting has always come into it somewhere. For me, ordination is a deepening of or a seal on what I already am. If, in this context, I feel negative about parish ministry for all kinds of reasons, isn't this an indication of the future? Being part of a clericalized ministry makes me very uneasy. I feel a bond with spiritually minded people, not the ecclesiastical elite. This is a distressing time because it is not at all what I expected to happen. I hope I can find the faith to see my way through this.

It's still most depressing. Everything seems to lose meaning because I am utterly displaced and despondent. I am also bored because, as a theology graduate, I have covered most of the curriculum in detail already. One of the staff says that preparing for priesthood is like watching grass grow. I am used to a more vibrant life—journalism is much more interactive and life-giving. I'm feeling nostalgic, and my mind is playing tricks on me. At one point today I felt sure I could see a journalist friend coming through the cloisters. My legs walked faster but my heart sank when I realized it was a student who just happened to look like him. It's all about illusion and reality here. A ray of hope beams into my life when I meet a priest from outside the community who seems to know about displacement and training. "It's all so very religious, isn't it?" he says. This is precisely the point. It's more about religion than spirituality.

I arrange to meet the priest to gain some information for a project I am undertaking on ministry. It is the only assignment here that remotely interests me. As I have taken my tape recorder to the college (like all good seminarians), I can't wait to resuscitate it. The priest looks a little surprised when my informal chat with him is transformed into a full-scale interview. I begin by asking him when he first discovered "he had a vocation to something." It is the sort of question that he finds almost impossible to answer. He first raised the matter of becoming a priest when he was eleven but "I really only think I said that because I wanted to please the curate who asked me." He adds that there must have been "some latent sense of God calling me. I was responding to a call without knowing what I was doing so, which is rather the way God works." As he relates his story, I sense connections with my own. I am curious to know how he was able to distinguish between being called to live a deeper Christian witness and being called to be a priest. "That's a very big question," he acknowledges, then continues:

> It's part of the scandal of particularity. Everyone who is a Christian has a vocation. But within that wide sense is the particular way in which God calls each person. God himself is a very particular God. He calls you and he calls me. He's calling everybody. One of the significant factors about prayer is the profoundly personal nature of God's relationship with each one of us. We are unique in the eyes of God. No one person has the same vocation as another. We might have a common vocation as priests, shall we say, but you only have to live in a theological college for a few minutes to discover there is an infinite variety of priesthoods—as many, in a sense, as there are priests.

Do some people become priests because of the expectations of others? The priest answers at length:

> All our lives we are trying to live up to other people's expectations—that's one of the tragedies. All through our school days, people are loading us with their expectations and sometimes shrouding the true expectation which is God's expectation of us. If we do break away and try to live up to the divine expectation, how many disasters come in its train? How many men and women have become monks or nuns in the teeth of vast opposition from families? Or priests? "Why when he read law has he gone into the priesthood? He could be earning

three times that much by now. He was bound to become a judge. Why has he thrown away his life?"

The "will of God" is a strange phrase because the word *will* comes from an amalgam of the Greek and the Hebrew, meaning "yearning on our part, yearning on God's." Should God's yearning for us conform with our particular yearning for God in our own ministry? "Thou wouldst not seek me if thou hadst not already found me" is such an important little saying in my life because, in the end, how can we possibly absolutely know God's will for us? We can become conscious of his yearning for us, and so our yearning for him really begins to conform to his yearning for us the more we look away from ourselves. "Our hearts are restless until they find their rest in Thee."

All the great people of prayer—the Curé d'Ars, St. Vincent de Paul, St. Francis of Assisi—were concerned only with God's expectations. In prayer we would long to aim for the point where our hearts beat with the same rhythm as God's heart. At that point you would cease to notice it was happening. We only notice it's there because we are out of synchronicity. But once your heart is really beating the same beat as God's heart, your life is hidden with Christ in God. That doesn't mean to say you lose yourself. It's not an obliteration of self. The more we learn to pray, the more uniquely ourselves we become. It's all a huge paradox.

The priest's words uplifted me for a while but now, after a weekend away, I am back in the grip of depression and the

dark night of St. John of the Cross gets blacker. Is this how
he felt when he was imprisoned? The mystical doctor composed great poetry in jail—I can hardly bring myself to write
in this journal. My creativity has been sapped. I feel ener-
vated. My vocation is dying. A light has gone out. In the last
ten days I haven't had the energy to write. Everyone seems to
say "hang in there," but all the inner feelings seem to suggest
this would be destructive. I am indifferent about almost
everything. I want to escape but not let anyone down. I think
that has been the problem: always living up to other people's
expectations.

I have had another bad night of dark dreams—wrestling
nightmares. Whatever is happening, it's giving me a good
shake up! God has felt distant these past few weeks, although
I did sense his presence at Compline (Night Prayer) yesterday. I still see myself on the threshold. I am suspicious of
some people in the church. I feel mentally and spiritually
drained at times, bored with religion and uninspired by what
I read. I was more in touch with my spirituality when I was
on the news desk. I still think the Church has hijacked the
notion of vocation—a "calling" is interpreted as a calling to
priesthood. We assume that's what vocation is because no
one in the Church ever suggests it could be a calling to something else. In my case, I wonder if it was a calling to healing.
I have taken part in healing services; my dreams about ministry have, on the whole, had a healing theme; and my pull
toward priesthood has often been about the sick. I sense
some deeper truth in what I have just written.

It is six o'clock and I have woken early after a dream in
which I was apparently a deacon in a black cassock back at

the church where I grew up. I had to sort out something trivial, such as attending to the photocopier or to the parish magazine, or answering the door to someone from the parish. I felt ill at ease and infantilized. I had been ordained but didn't much care for it. It all seemed so banal, as if my years of experience counted for nothing. I felt controlled, under somebody else's thumb.

Yesterday I looked at the story of Elijah. "What are you doing here?" God asks him on a mountain—it's a question I might well ask myself. But Elijah doesn't find God through the wind, earthquake, and fire that follow. He has to wait for the still small voice. Elijah goes back, so should I? In the book *Being a Priest Today*, which I forced myself to glance at, a contributor says it is the job of the laity to play out its ministry in the world—home, work, and society— "Each person must work with the gifts, talents, deficiencies, handicaps, and graces they receive to bring about the kingdom through the action of the Holy Spirit." Citing communications media as one example, he goes on to say that the church has never given enough support to those who have "a very clear task in the kingdom being realized out there." This is priestliness—the abundance of grace, proclaimed by Jesus, which we follow through the "daily sacrifice of mercy, justice, and love."[26]

I find it hard to write anything of significance, for I am utterly alienated from all this. I can find no reason for being here. I moved to a new room, which happened to be next to the fire escape. I might well make use of it. Like St. John of the Cross, I have often plotted my route in the night. "O that I had wings like a dove, to fly away and be at rest...." I do not want to join the clerics: it's as simple as that. Ten days ago I went to look around a large hospital with a view to a chaplaincy placement, but now I do not even have the drive to do that. I felt so depressed as I walked around the wards, which is completely out of character. I love visiting patients in the hospital, so what on earth is going on with me? The person I once was is disappearing. Perhaps it's the context I'm in. Meaninglessness. Depression. Boredom. Irritation. I have no interest in praying. No motivation. It is a form of death. I have loathed it since I arrived and see little point in continuing here. It's not *me*.

Having given up my job, there is nothing to return to. I have to move on in blind faith. But today, two months after arriving here, I decided to pull out of the course altogether. The college staff are understanding and supportive, so I knew my letter of resignation would not come as a complete surprise. As I placed the letter in the principal's pigeonhole, I reached down to mine and discovered an envelope with a BBC logo. It was from a colleague in the religious broadcasting department. Was I interested in a job as a producer? I could not believe what I was reading. I had written my resignation letter without any knowledge this was afoot. It seemed to be an extraordinary confirmation. I reflected on this for a day, then made contact with the BBC. I have an interview next Thursday. As Archbishop William Temple once said: "As long as the prayers go on, the coincidences continue." So it now seems that neither part-time nor full-time ministry was my calling. Three years ago tonight I had my car accident, which triggered my thoughts about institutional priesthood. Perhaps it was really a vocation to a deeper priestliness within me. Why should this sense of calling be any the less strong?

I was offered the job and today left the seminary. At the end of Morning Prayer and before the Eucharist, the principal bestowed on me a blessing. As I knelt before him, he prayed: "God, you have called Mike to be a journalist. Confirm in him that calling and, as he sets out from here on his new path, may his work reveal compassion, truth, hope, and justice."

I feel more at peace.

9

LUMINOUS GAZE

When you attain to the region of tears, then know that your mind has left the prison of this world and has set its foot on the roadway of the new age.

ISAAC THE SYRIAN

*W*orking now as a network producer and reporter, my vocation is back on track. I am constantly on the move around the United Kingdom and Ireland, and sometimes travel abroad. One minute I might be recording a sequence with Archbishop Desmond Tutu, the next interviewing the Reverend Jesse Jackson on a visit to London. Since leaving the seminary, I have continued to have vivid dreams in which I still pine about being a priest. Sometimes I have felt lifted up on shafts of light—experiences of an almost mystical nature too personal to share, as though my whole being were becoming God-fused.

Today I'm reporting from Belfast, Northern Ireland, and am remembering a conversation I had earlier with a fearless nun. Twenty-four years ago Sister Anna was sent to this divided city by her Anglican community. From her home on the borders, she built up remarkable relationships and was one of the founders of Northern Ireland's first ecumenical school. I became engrossed as she described the living-out of a vocation on the edge. I was naturally curious to find out

how Sister Anna became aware of her vocation and was
somewhat relieved to learn that it was a long and compli-
cated process. I am cautious of vocations that work out too
smoothly. Sister Anna told me that hers had begun very def-
initely, at a distinct moment in time, when she was five. Until
then she had never really "taken God in." She had "never
really noticed" God or looked at him. She remembered sitting on the knee of her father who was talking to her about
God. She "knew immediately" that God was God and that
God claimed her totally. Her words lingered in my memory
tonight:

> I think it's absolutely fantastic that some people
> can simply be created for God, not to be useful or
> serve any purpose unless he wants to use them in
> some way or another, but just as it were, out of his
> own sovereign will, he chooses them to be there for
> him and to write a blank check, which is what we
> do when we are professed, simply giving ourselves
> to God. He then takes it seriously and anything
> can happen. The very next day after your profes-
> sion, you can be struck down with deadly cancer
> and spend the rest of your monastic life dying.
> Anything that happens to you after your profes-
> sion is absolutely fine because the essence is that
> you have given yourself to God. He has taken you
> and is using you in any way he wants. Whatever
> way that is doesn't make the slightest difference.

This afternoon I'm exploring Sweden as part of a short
break from the journalistic frenzy. But I know from experience that sometimes my spiritual sojourning can be equally
eventful. During the entire four-hour journey north from the

capital, Stockholm, to the lakeside town of Mora, I read the psalms. I am due to take the *Inlandsbanan,* a scenic railway that curves through the mountains. As my train slows toward its destination, I look out from the window and notice a congregation of spruce trees, huddling between the track and the lake. I feel I have been here before, even though I know I haven't. The trees remind me of the front cover of one of my favorite texts: Henri Nouwen's *Reaching Out.* Funnily enough it's three years to the day since I interviewed him. Then I begin to suspect that something is about to happen. I have no idea precisely what, of course, but it is as though I am waiting in the wings. I am so convinced of the significance of the trees that I ask a fellow passenger to take a picture of me looking out at them through the carriage window.

At Mora I get out of the train and proceed to the ticket office to find out about the mountain railway connection, only to learn that the service has been wound up for the summer. So I head off and find a hotel in the town, a much smaller place than I had anticipated and a lot quieter. In fact, the silence perturbs me. To my right, I pass a large Lutheran church—it is the day the Lutheran Church in Sweden is splitting from the state—and feel drawn toward it. Through the windows I can see a candelabra flickering—almost beckoning. It is so quiet, and I intuit something afoot about my vocation. I wander into the church and, like a detective, hunt for a clue as to why I have felt so compelled to enter. I look around, then behind the altar, I notice a reredos of the Last Supper. The luminous eyes of Christ are jewels that gaze, not so much at me, but *into* me. They are knowing, longing, and loving. I feel searched out:

> O LORD, you have searched me and known me.
> You know when I sit down and when I rise up;
>   you discern my thoughts from far away.
> You search out my path and my lying down,
>   and are acquainted with all my ways.

Even before a word is on my tongue,
   O LORD, you know it completely.
You hem me in, behind and before,
   and lay your hand upon me.
Such knowledge is too wonderful for me;
   it is so high that I cannot attain it.
Where can I go from your spirit?
   Or where can I flee from your presence?

(Ps 139)

The eyes seem to say, "You are a priest forever after the order of Melchizedek" (the priest and king of Salem who had met and blessed Abraham on his journey into the unknown). Tears flow naturally. The priesthood of the whole people of God is the priesthood after the order of Melchizedek.

But is this experience really of Christ or is it the devil playing Christ?

I prostrate myself in front of the altar. I then get up and rummage in my haversack for a prayer book. I read the Magnificat to an empty church, turning to the altar for the doxology. The eyes are still looking at me and I feel slightly uncomfortable. What is this about? I get the impression that the encounter is about my calling. I look down at the ring that I placed on my finger on Mount Teide. As I leave the church, disturbed, I can still feel the eyes, penetrating and loving. They seem to say "Will you?" but, after all that has gone before, how do I know it's not my imagination? I feel calmer, yet stunned, as I walk through the town. As I reflect beside the lake, I ask a passerby to take another picture for the record. The town seems to have a personal significance for me. As I walk back into a precinct, I observe a black statue of St. Michael slaying the dragon and subsequently learn that the town is dedicated to St. Michael, who at one time (although not now) was patron saint of the Church. I go to the library to discover that the word *Mora* means "swampy land out of which the spruces grow."

After a night of disturbing dreams, I return to the Lutheran church to say my prayers—the eyes on the altar still penetrate. I decide to seek out the local Lutheran priest. He listens intently, asking if I sensed evil when I went into the church. Were the eyes loving? How did I feel after it had happened? He tells me not to be frightened by it but to feel blessed. He senses it has been an important experience and is pleased I have told him about it. It might not have to do with priesthood, he concludes, but also possibly about bringing people to the Eucharist. He says the sense of fear I felt is like an episode from the Old Testament prophets. Before I leave, he gives me a blessing in Swedish. I do not know the words he used but I often wonder what he said.

I have discussed the experience with a spiritual guide who points out that the path to God is one of peace and tranquility, not worry and anxiety. I should rightly question it, move into prayer with it, but not look at it intensely. I should shift the anxiety out of it. Emotions are valuable but can get out of hand and cloud common sense.

Four days later and I find myself at the former Nazi concentration camp of Auschwitz, Poland. I'm accompanying the chief rabbi of the United Hebrew Congregation of the Commonwealth on his first visit here. With him is a personal protection officer whose grandparents were murdered at Auschwitz. He obtains copies of their registration here. I am profoundly moved by Auschwitz, especially when I come across the children's clothing starkly displayed behind glass cabinets—booties, little trousers, socks, and shoes, not to mention a mountain of suitcases. It might be a journalistic assignment, but it is a spiritual privilege to be here. On our way back to Warsaw Airport, the chief rabbi deepens my understanding of uniqueness when he comments: "The prophets aren't bothered about conventions. Their concern is to communicate truth." Is my own role in life more prophetic than priestly perhaps? We stop off on the outskirts of Kalice to remember the 140 Jews killed in a pogrom after the Holocaust. The chief rabbi looks across the fields and sings a prayer for the dead. I am blessed to be part of this pilgrimage.

My life glides from one journalistic experience to another. There is hardly time to absorb their psychological and spiritual impact. Back in London, I am now on a controversial assignment about cults, which is stirring up people's emotions. En route to my hotel, I notice that the driver is quiet. He asks me what I do. This leads to his saying that faith doesn't mean anything to him anymore. We talk about authority figures in the Church and about our images of God. Then he discloses that his nephew was killed in a car crash seven months ago. As a result, his parents have found it difficult to have faith. The nephew was twenty-four, a good lad, he says. The family has had a tough time. I share this burden for a while. As I get out, the driver says he's never opened up to a passenger before but feels better for having spoken. I tell him I'll light a candle for the family and his nephew in church tomorrow and keep him in my prayers. As I unlock the door to my hotel room, frazzled after a relentless day chasing a dubious story, I realize there must be so many people like the taxi driver, who've abandoned institutional religion or never been attracted to it, yet are yearning for someone with whom they can talk through deep questions of belief.

❧

I am in northern Britain, today reporting on the work of a homeless center attached to a cathedral. The eyes of one man I interview are Christ-like. Perhaps they remind me of the altarpiece at the Lutheran church in Sweden. The man speaks about death and of his contempt for alcohol. There is sadness in his appearance but I strongly sense Christ in him. His words conclude my broadcast. This voice for the voiceless will be heard by over a million listeners.

Through these many and varied experiences, I am gaining a deeper understanding of my spiritual pilgrimage. The assignments can change as dramatically as the scenery in which they are located. One minute I am on the rugged island of Iona following in the footsteps of St. Columba off the west coast of Scotland, the next hearing the disturbing story of a Roman Catholic priest who says he will be psychologically scarred for the rest of his life as a result of the way in which he claims the Church betrayed him. I decide to ask this man how he would now define the word *priest*. He replies, "A priest is someone who, in her or his friendship, reveals to me the face of God." I have also received a letter from a former Trappist monk, now a mail carrier in the States. He says he has "moved from seeking the presence of God in the monastery to becoming the presence of God in the world."

That is a priestly vocation.

10

REQUIEM

Let the eternal dawn break for them...
FROM A TRADITIONAL CHRISTIAN PRAYER

I am on an assignment that is putting the spiritual and journalistic within me to their severest test. As I help set up a makeshift editing suite in a remote Scottish farmhouse, I know the task ahead will be grim. Sixteen children and their teacher have been massacred in their primary school in the small city of Dunblane. I am here to report on it. But I also desire a pastoral role to be alongside this community in its grief. As I stand beside a row of tabloid photographers, perched on step ladders, I remember what one of them said to me over breakfast in the farmhouse kitchen: "I couldn't possibly cry when I'm on these jobs. You can't take pictures if you have tears in your eyes." But he is an exception. The tragedy is affecting the most brazen of journalists, especially those with young families.

As television satellite dishes are being mounted outside the school gates, I know that getting people to talk will be the main challenge, especially as the emotions and patience of the shocked community already seem to have been worn down by the early news teams. It is virtually impossible to contact any priest or minister on the phone, and there is a weary exasperation in the voices of those housekeepers, secretaries, and spouses on constant answering duty. I know I have to show up on the doorstep of local clergy. They might then put me in touch with people who have close connections with the school. So it is with some anxiety that I make my way to the local Roman Catholic church, which is unlocked so that people could go inside and pray. I hope I might run into the parish priest, but there is no sign of him. A staircase leads me to an upper room. As I peer around an open door, my eyes focus on a small group of men, all wearing black ties. At the sight of me, their tone lowers and they frown. After exchanging a few words, one of them says, "I think you should go."

I am ushered out of the building swiftly. One of my escorts asks some parishioners where the priest is, but they shrug their shoulders. It seems people aren't going to say, even if they know. The following morning I turn up again at the church, just as people are leaving Mass. Recognizing me from the night before, a parishioner says firmly, "We don't want any of this." She makes it clear she wants me to move away at once. I explain that I'm keen to speak with someone connected with the school. Her eyes glance at the person beside her—who just happens to be the school's Catholic religious education specialist. More significantly, Anne taught two of the boys who died. Early indications suggest she will grant an interview but, as we walk toward a car where a friend was waiting, she starts to have second thoughts and asks if she can discuss the proposal with the friend. Anne soon comes back over to me and says, "She doesn't think I should do it." But I sense Anne *will* speak so long as she has the support of someone else. She decides to go to the rectory. After a while, she returns with the priest's blessing. It is a naturally difficult interview but she answers every question from the heart. By the end she is clearly emotionally exhausted and upset; there are tears in my eyes too. I know that I have been fortunate in securing a moving and exclusive interview for radio and, to my surprise, Anne says she was glad she had done it. The conversation has actually helped to put a myriad of thoughts and feelings into some shape for the first time since the shootings. And, strangely, it has been a journalist, rather than a priest, who has allowed this to happen.

Later that day, I strike up a conversation with another local resident who works as a pizza chef in the town. It turns out that Pierre happens to live in the same house as a family who've lost their daughter—his flat is directly beneath theirs. I ask if he will record an interview in the street and he agrees. But, embarrassingly, I can't get my tape recorder to work. After putting in new batteries, we agree to go back to his flat to try the recording again in the peace of his home. But after four further attempts, the machine is still acting up. When Pierre attempts to answer the same sensitive question for the fifth time, he is just too traumatized to continue. Before completing the interview, we start praying together and say the Our Father. It is rare for such spiritual bonding to impact on journalistic situations but in Dunblane it seems the natural, priestly, thing to do.

That evening, for the first time in my life, I see people lining up to go to church. The long line into the vigil service stretches from the cathedral entrance, through the graveyard, and right down the hill into the center of the city. For radio reports, it is essential to gather what's known as "actuality"—real-life sound effects that create atmosphere and give a sense of place. Earlier in the day, I gained permission from church officials to record parts of the service but now, as I squeeze past people at the door and explain where I am from, a steward makes it clear that I am far from welcome. "We've not been told you're coming. You can't come inside. In any case, there isn't room." As he speaks, the crowd surges forward, pushing me to one side. I feel spectacularly in the way. The steward's looks and comments underscore my acute embarrassment. Far from comfortable with my role, I eventually manage to get into the cathedral and position myself in front of a pillar. As the organist begins a sequence of reflective music, I switch on my recorder. But the cathedral staff look aghast, and a minister signals to turn it off. I attempt to indicate that I have permission but, in the emotional bewilderment of the night, it is impossible to communicate the message clearly. The minister asks me to leave, her left arm pointing to the door. I know what she must be thinking and, while I feel awkward, I am also irritated because I genuinely want to be there to pray with those people. I state I would really like to stay. I put the recorder on pause and retreat behind the pillar. But the minister suspects I am secretly recording, and she insists I switch off the machine completely. Her misgivings are, however, understandable. On the day of the shootings, one tabloid reporter turned up at the house of a bereaved family at a quarter to midnight—and was chased away by a distraught father.

I stay conspicuously behind my pillar, seemingly caught between two worlds. I know that the producers expect "actuality" of the service. But I am aware also that I have to be with that community in a deeper way. After standing for nearly an hour, I ask if I can sit in the pew. "You don't have to ask permission for that," the minister retorts. So, with my tape recorder resting by the pillar, I sit down and write her a note on the back of my business card, explaining the predicament. I pass it across, watch her read it, and immediately notice a change of attitude. She quickly comes over and says quietly, "We're all on a short fuse. Carry on recording." I go to take the card from her, but she says she wants to keep it "to remind me of my bad temper." Shortly afterwards, she walks back again to my pew, takes my hand, and holds it for ten minutes. A night of tense misunderstanding is transformed, all the more poignant in the context of the somber liturgy. It is an experience of reconciliation I shall never forget, sacramental in its intensity.

While journalists often have privileged access, it is sometimes necessary for them to stop and consider the ethical demarcation lines, especially when intruding into somebody's—or some community's—grief or misfortune. At times of tragedy, we can be among the first on the scene, sometimes arriving before the priest. While Dunblane is proving to be a particularly delicate situation, it often surprises me how open people are to the media in tragic circumstances. We are allowed into their lives to share their fears and confusion. Sometimes we even receive letters of thanks, not for what we reported, but for the personal words we offer at the time. These vulnerable moments carry the risk of exploitation, and much depends on trust. But if we choose to be compassionate, they can become holy encounters within a hidden ministry of priestly journalism.

However, all of us face dilemmas with which to test our ultimate loyalties. What happens if we stumble across a scandal involving people in our own faith community? Dare we keep silent at the next editorial meeting among colleagues who expect us to have good religious contacts? Or if we are interviewing a weeping mother whose son has been killed in headline-making circumstances, do we keep the tape recorder running because the sound of crying makes good radio—or do we turn it off and put our pastoral convictions before our journalistic instincts?

The Catholic journalist Clifford Longley, who once said he was paid to keep an open mind, has also struggled with this question of identity. One possible solution, he considered, was to split himself in two: becoming the neutral and detached observer by day and the dedicated person with a cause by night. But he found that the detachment of the professional followed him home, and there were always two sides to every question, even in the privacy of his own thoughts. And he also came to see that "priest" was a description we all take on at certain times in certain roles, when circumstances demand that we should be an instrument of the sacred.

The late Gerald Priestland, who worked as a religious correspondent for the BBC, believed that, despite its shortcomings and its failures, its blemishes and its disgraces, journalism could be a Christian calling. He also felt that the best journalism had "something in common with poetry: its compression, its rhythm, its evocative use of language to draw the listener in, its treatment of language as if it were a sacrament."[27] While some journalists have quit newsrooms to train as priests and some priests have left the Church to follow new callings in journalism, I remain convinced that the world of journalism does indeed present its own priestly work that would not otherwise come my way. The sacred art of reporting is about holding all these paradoxes in creative tension and discovering the compassion of God at the cutting edge of current affairs.

The experiences of other people's journeys lead us closer to the heart of our own.

11

SILENT MUSIC

He collects the waves of the ocean...
he stores up the depths of the sea.
PSALM 33:7

*I*t is a gloriously warm July day here on the coast of northeastern Spain. I am writing this at the cove of Garraf on a canopied terrace overlooking the glistening Mediterranean. After ordering a bottle of chilled white wine, my traveling companion and I get on with our holiday reading. As my friend produces Brian Moore's *No Other Life* from his sports bag, I open my haversack and expose to the heat a small hardback edition of *The Music of Silence,* an invitation to enter "the sacred space of monastic experience." Authored by the Benedictine monk David Steindl-Rast, it had been written as a companion to *Chant,* the best-selling recording by the Benedictine monks of Santo Domingo di Silos in Spain. The book illustrates how the monastic hours are divine messengers, everyday angels that announce the gifts and challenges of each part of the day.

The book was mailed to me from the States a few weeks ago by Robert Durback, the friend who left monastic life after fourteen years to become a postman. He has always amused me in his letters by implying that, while I might think of myself as a journalist, I am really "a monk at heart." A description of his own transition helped me understand the

nature of "secular" vocation—his own personal challenge
had been trying to integrate his new life as a mail carrier on
foot, with his past life as a contemplative on his knees: "In
the monastery my focus was on seeking God. But as a letter
carrier, walking from house to house and family to family,
my vocation was no longer to seek the presence of God but
to become the presence of God—far more demanding."

My journalistic colleagues sometimes joke that they
would never be surprised to hear that I have fled to a
monastery. I suppose the monastic influence was there from
the start. I was born in a maternity home on the site of a one-
time Augustinian friary and grew up on land that once
formed part of its estate. One of my earliest experiences of
monasticism was as a callow reporter when I went to interview the prior of the Community of the Glorious Ascension,
who lived in a converted barn close to the coast. The published article was headlined "Trying to Be a Light in a Dark
Corner." It was my first serious piece of so-called religious
journalism and I still vividly remember the interview. In a
strange way, I felt connected with the community's life, and I
spent much longer with them than research for the article
really justified. Nobody had asked me to do the story. It was
a neat diversion from the tedious council-committee skir-
mishes to which members of the journalistic novitiate were
inevitably sent. "We are successors to the apostles and com-
mitted to Christ," the bald prior told me. "We are not escaping from the world. We pray for it."

I remember his telling me that it had been such a relief
to him to find a reporter who "was willing to share himself
as well as extract information about someone else." Kind
though they were, his words momentarily troubled me. I was
only nineteen at the time and suddenly wondered if I had
broken a journalistic commandment by opening up spiritually with a person I had just interviewed. As I reflected, I
began to ponder on whether I might have a vocation, not to
be a monk or a priest, but to be a journalist of the spiritual.

Those early signs of discernment are playing back in my mind today as the Spanish waiter uncorks the bottle and pours wine into the glass. But I hardly notice him. I have become so absorbed in *The Music of Silence* that the din of the crowded resort seems like a track from a BBC sound-effects CD. Each chapter is named for one of the liturgical hours, or monastic season of the day: "Vigils: The Night Watch," "Lauds: The Coming of the Light," "Prime: Deliberate Beginning," "Terce: Blessing," "Sext: Fervor and Commitment," "None: Shadows Grow Longer," "Vespers: Lighting the Lamps," "Compline: Completing the Circle," and "The Great Silence: The Matrix of Time."

As I turn the pages and savor every sentence, I become entranced by the rhythms of the monastic day and then mysteriously start to relive my career as a journalist. The descriptions of each season suddenly evoke powerful images of my struggle to report and to pray, to search for truth without and within. I have always remembered that Thomas Merton described himself as a journalist because he was "one who observed." Here, in the afternoon heat of a picturesque Spanish resort, I scribble "The Journalist and the Monk" on the opening page of a notebook, with the subtitle "A Spirituality of Listening and Seeing." More than anything I have ever read, *The Music of Silence* is helping me to understand the uniqueness of my vocation. The journalist, I write, is trained to see what others don't, to make connections, to hear what isn't being said. The monk, on the other hand, as the book explains, is called to perceive "what eye has not seen nor ear heard." Within the next few hours I consider comparisons between the two lifestyles, such as the prerequisite of being vigilant at all times, as well as the discipline (on an early-news work shift) of getting out of bed at half-past three in the morning and spending the first half hour of the day in prayer. This was something I had tried to live up to during those grueling years of bulletin preparation and delivery in my years as a news anchor. There is also a connection between the monk's control of his breathing for chanting and the broadcaster's skill in having to breathe in a disciplined way when news-reading.

But there are also big differences, such as the stability of the monastic life contrasted with the nomadic and somewhat rootless nature of media work. Furthermore, there is the matter of time. For David Steindl-Rast, the central message of monasticism is the supreme importance of time. Chant music conjures the archetype of the monk's harmonious way of life: the time available is in proportion to the task in hand. Every page of the book seems to have a message for the journalist in me:

> Saturated with information but often bereft of meaning, we feel caught in a never-ending swirl of duties and demands, things to finish, things to put right. Yet as we dart anxiously from one activity to the next, we sense that there is more to life than our worldly agendas.
>
> Our uneasiness and our frantic scrambling are caused by our distorted sense of time, which seems to be continually running out. Western culture reinforces this misconception of time as a limited commodity: We are always meeting *dead*lines; we are always short on time, we are always running out of time.[28]

Studying the book, it becomes apparent that, at a deep level, my natural impulses resonate more with the monastic temperament than the journalistic psyche, even though I have no question in my mind that my own vocation has always been journalistic rather than monastic. Steindl-Rast believes calling and responding belong to the essence of chant. He also acknowledges the shadow side of vocation:

We all struggle with dark periods, like Jacob wrestling in the night with the Divine Presence in the form of a dark angel, beautiful and yet terrifying. At the end of the night, the angel says, "Let me go." But Jacob replies, "I will not let you go unless you bless me." As dawn breaks, the angel blesses him, but also injures him by touching his thigh. From that day on, Jacob limps. There is a mysterious woundedness that somehow goes with great blessing.

When we truly encounter the night in all its beauty and terror, we have no assurance whatsoever that we are going to come out unscathed. If you come out injured, it might just be a sign of the blessing that you have received there.[29]

Pitched against the rock-face of a serrated mountain, the monastery I'm now visiting is an oasis of meditative spirituality. The offices in native Catalan are sung with prayerful beauty. The Friday-evening Eucharist is celebrated in a modern side-chapel in front of a chiseled statue of the wounded Christ. The priest is heavenly in his gestures. His words, had they been understood, would have been uplifting, but his manner of speaking them is effective enough. I awake at six this morning to stroll around this stunning setting, then at a quarter to seven watch the sun rise. It is like a host being lifted up.

The morning office and conventual Mass are serenely celebrated, while the calm comings and goings of the monks beneath the venerated statue of the Black Madonna are spiritual movements in themselves, ordered and hopeful, but not affected. I have been reading Esther de Waal's book *Seeking God,* about the Way of St. Benedict. It exposes the folly of working too hard and of not bringing a balance into situations. She writes: "We are all essentially rhythmic creatures—

life needs this rhythm and balance if it is to be consistently good and not drain us from the possibility of being or becoming our whole selves." Later, she explains that the idea of Benedictine equilibrium is not an end in itself. "It is a means for total integration…so that a more complete experience of God becomes possible."[30] I know I must heed her words. They remind me of a convent poster of a panda chewing a bamboo shoot: "Relax—God's in charge."

After lunch, I take the St. Joan funicular railway to the top and follow a medieval pilgrim route to the hermitage of St. Michael, my patron saint. I feel I had to do this. There was something for me there. The chapel was locked but through an iron gate I spy an altar. Above and behind it is a fresco of the archangel Michael triumphing over the evil forces. I throw money into the chapel as others have done before. I pray here for St. Michael to give me strength and guide me—to sort out my contradictions. Later as I pass St. Michael's Cross, I notice the words on the monastery gate: *Ste. Michael Archangele, Defende nos in praelio.* Archangel St. Michael, protect us with your prayers.

I have come back to the now-deserted stretch of beach alone. It is early morning. As waves crash against the rocks and the thrusting foam glistens, I become aware of my utter insignificance. Yet once I have accepted and am able to hold on to that awareness, I feel more at peace with myself and more conscious of the natural world around me: footprints in the wet solid sand, a solitary feather lying near a dead gull, a multicolored shell prized open like butterfly wings, a dented beer can washed up like a wreck. On the beach I detect life and death, beauty and abandonment. The waves and the sun breaking through the overcast skies create their own purification rite. I'm sitting beneath the railway line beside a row of white and green Catalonian beach homes.

There have been periods of darkness and loneliness this week, but here on this shoreline again I feel renewed by the tranquility of the place, the music of the sea, and the still-ness (and deeper stillness) that such an atmosphere evokes. I wake monastically at 3:30 this morning after a disturbing dream about demons. I think the dark makes us easy prey to their attack. I read Psalm 16, which brings a sense of peace and divine protection. Now I can continue the retreat as a sort of cleansing from those nightmares. This morning's Gospel explains that "it is the spirit which brings light." The waves soothe as you jettison the past into the sea—as though the waters cleanse the soul and refreshment comes with the tide.

The sea puts me in touch with my *being*. Deserted beaches are places of mystery, paradox, and vulnerability. The Nebraskan naturalist Loren Eiseley, who once lived in a seaside town, would spend the early morning walking the beach because he couldn't sleep. Every day, as the sun was rising, he watched local people combing the sand for starfish that had been washed ashore the previous night. The objec-tive was to kill the fish and sell them. For Eiseley it was an indication of all the ways the world says no to life. One morning he got up earlier than usual and spotted a solitary figure on the beach, gathering the starfish. But as he watched, Eiseley noticed that each time the man found one alive he would pick it up and throw it as far as he could back into the ocean from whence it had originated. Eiseley discov-ered that this man undertook his missions of mercy every day of the week. He called him "the star thrower." The man's work contradicted everything that Eiseley had been taught about evolution and the survival of the fittest. There, on the beach, the strong reached down, not to crush, but to save the weak. Eiseley wondered: Is there a star thrower at work in the universe, a God who contradicts death, a God whose nature is (in the words of Thomas Merton) "mercy within mercy within mercy?"[31]

The shoreline always reveals to us our deeper motivations, a place from which we gain insight at times of inner change. It can also feed our moods. I once worked for a newspaper a few miles from the sea. The copy editor, whose own marriage had broken up, veered at times toward depression and was not always an easy person to deal with. For months I noticed that he would disappear from the office at lunchtime with his thermos and sandwiches, rather than join the rest of us for a bowl of soup in the local pub. He later told me that, every day, he felt compelled to drive to the nearest beach and have his lunch by the water. He needed to look out onto the distant waves and reflect on his life. This daily meditation, alone on the flat sands, was essential therapy. He always seemed in a better mood in the afternoons.

The coast is unpretentious territory where we sometimes face uneasy truths about ourselves and ponder eternal verities. There is a real sense of being connected to the elements and caught up in the life of the God of the universe. The repetitive sound of the waves echo the underlying spiritual thrust—that God is a loving and humble creator who can speak to me through the rhythms of the day. The sea evokes—more than symbolizes—God's yearning for us. It is a grand gesture but also a vulnerable one.

Like the ocean, the love of God is steadfast, yet always surging.

12

HEAVENLY MELODIES

Be joyful, seek the best, and let the sparrows chirp.

POPE JOHN XXIII

*E*very night, as I break bread under a starlit sky for the morrow's dawn choristers, I feel I am participating in a eucharistic act. I remember the words of a hospital chaplain who incorporated these words during the Mass:

> Be gentle when you touch Bread.
> Let it not lie uncared for,
> Unwanted.
> So often Bread is taken for granted.
> There is such beauty in Bread.
> Beauty of Sun and Soil,
> Beauty of patient toil.
> Wind and rain have caressed it,
> Christ often blessed it.
> Be gentle when you touch Bread.

I feel I am a mere note in the vast melody of creation, contributing, in the words of St. Athanasius, to "an exquisite single euphonious harmony." God holds the universe "like a lyre," drawing together "the things in the air with those on earth, and those in the heaven with those in the air...."[32] In one of his hymns, St. Ephrem the Syrian compares the growth of faith to that of a bird. He observes that, in order for the bird to fly, it has to open its wings "in the symbol of the Cross." He then adds:

> But if the bird gathers in its wings,
> thus denying the extended symbol of the Cross,
> then the air too will deny the bird:
> the air will not carry the bird
> unless its wings confess the Cross.[33]

Birds are integral to my spiritual pilgrimage and often my notes in this journal reflect occasions when I have been mesmerized by their glorious song. This evening, for example, as I was heading out into the country, I noticed a winged chorister perched on the pinnacle of an old school. The bird's message was a celestial hymn of purity and joy. The melody seemed unending and I stood entranced, lifted up into the birdsong. It spoke of the risk we all have to take if we are to be true to our uniqueness. It is about daring to be different.

On the front cover of a small Bible I take with me on my travels, I have glued a postcard of Picasso's *Los Pichones* (the Pigeons) which he painted in the South of France. In the picture, white figures peck at seeds in an alcove above a blue Mediterranean. On the back cover I have pasted a paper icon of St. Francis preaching to the birds, looked on by "Brother Sun." An owl is perched on his left hand and a pigeon, with one wing outstretched, rests on his left shoulder. To the left is a congregation of birds. These creatures teach me all I need to know about divine calling. Commenting on St. Francis in one of his encyclical letters, Pope John Paul the Second says the friar looked upon creation with the eyes of one who could recognize in it "the marvelous work of the hand of God." His voice, his glance, and his solicitous care toward human beings, animals, and nature are a faithful echo of the love with which God in the beginning brought them into

existence. The pontiff says we too are called to a similar attitude. Created in the image of God, we must make God present among creatures "as intelligent and noble masters and
guardians of nature and not as heedless exploiters and
destroyers."[34]

I'm thinking back to one afternoon when I was about
twelve. I came cheerfully home from school, only to find our
blue parakeet lying dead at the bottom of the cage with his
green-feathered companion standing over him, quivering,
perplexed, and grief-stricken. There Bobby stayed, beside
the body of Flinty, faithfully and silently, unable to compre-
hend what had happened. It was a tableau of pathos, for
they had been the best of pals and earlier that day had been
chattering as usual on their perches. Then, without warning,
Flinty suffered a heart attack and died instantly. Bobby must
have jumped down swiftly and hastened across the sandpa-
per to be alongside. After we removed Flinty from the cage
and buried him in the garden, Bobby ruffled up his feathers
and perched himself in the corner. He was clearly in mourn-
ing, facing bereavement alone. Such was his sorrow that he
had not the energy to peck at his seeds or lower his beak
into water. Two days later he too died, presumably of a broken heart. It was my first encounter with death, and I have
never forgotten it. The memory reminds me of the divine
calling to stand alongside and love vulnerably. As Henri
Nouwen puts it: "Life is precious. Not because it is
unchangeable like a diamond but because it is vulnerable
like a little bird. To love life means to love its vulnerability,
asking for care, attention, guidance, and support. Life and
death are connected by vulnerability."[35]

The American contemplative Thomas Merton understood the spirituality of birds. His hermitage was often encir-
cled in birdsong, and he used to interrupt his meditations to
watch savannah sparrows outside his bedroom window. He
wrote that at Thanksgiving he was grateful for the appearance of a little bird whose three notes "contained and

summed up all the melodies in the world." A whistling quail has "the sound of perfect innocence." For him, these hunted creatures were signs of life, gentleness, helplessness, providence, and love. He wrote about the gold vest of the meadowlark sitting on a fence post in the dawn sun, of flycatchers shaking their wings after the rain, and the cry of blue jays in the cedars, not to mention the worlds of the woodpecker, white crane, and myrtle warble. For him, each creature is a word of God.[36]

At her home in South Africa, Peggy Potgieter has lived close to birds. Ceres is a country town in the heart of a lush fruit-growing valley in the Western Cape where Peggy, her husband, George, and their three daughters have spent most of their lives, their home being a hub of love and hospitality in this multiracial community.

Peggy keeps two inverted ploughshares constantly filled with "Adam's ale"—water—one on the front lawn and the other on the back. One New Year's Eve, late in the afternoon, she cleaned the container at the back and filled it with fresh water, thinking how pleased the birds would be to have a New Year's drink. Waking early, she lifted the window blind to behold a beautiful turtledove sitting on the edge of the ploughshare.

> As I watched him, I was filled with delight, knowing how happy he would be. This little dove looked around him—most probably to see if all was well and that no cats or dogs were in the vicinity—then leaned forward, submerging his beak completely. He drank the water, long and deeply. I marveled at God's creation. The very next moment, this dear little dove rose into the air and swooped up, round and bang!—right into my kitchen window, in front of my eyes. I saw it falling and I rushed outside to try to save him. He was sitting all hunched up. I realized he was seri-

ously injured when he allowed me to pick him up ever so gently. I put him down in a safe place where our dogs wouldn't chase or disturb him. But five minutes later he just quietly lay on his side and died. I was most, most upset—and still am. This incident has stayed in my mind. It seems to be so meaningful for me and yet, what? What does it say?

The South African priest-poet Harry Wiggett draws inspiration from the life and death of birds:

Descending Dove, you were not here last year:
Now tell when, when did you first appear?
    I've always been eternal but of late
    I've left the heav'ns becoming incarnate.
Pray tell me why it is that you do sing
And soar about on lifting liquid wing?
    I've got a song to sing of godly love
    And future realms for man evolved above.
What is the meaning of your song, your plan
For falling failing wilderness-bound man?
    I sing forgiveness—that is why I live:
    And through my death I do forgiveness give.
    And from the grave I plan to rise, to fly
    Forever, that you man no more may die![37]

Harry tells me that when he and his wife, Jean, were engaged to be married, they went to a jeweler in Cape Town to choose their wedding rings. When selecting the one Jean was to give her fiancé, the jeweler asked if he had a family crest. When Harry explained he was not aware that he had one, the jeweler hauled out a great tome and, after searching through it, found the Wiggett family crest. It featured the dove returning to Noah with the olive branch in its beak. "It was such a wonderful affirmation from God of the marriage we were about to make," says Harry.

However, the dove was to have even greater theological significance after Harry moved to a new parish. Before he had even arrived, he was told that "the Spirit had come" there. "Because I did not fall into the exuberant ways of charismatic worship...a group of parishioners actually petitioned my bishop to have me removed, but he refused," Harry goes on. "One morning, when I was feeling particularly down in spirit, I went into the church and, as I sat quietly in the chapel where the Blessed Sacrament was reserved, I suddenly became aware of a dove cooing in the garden outside: 'I love you. I love you. I love you.' The Lord had spoken! And in that moment of hearing, my depression caused by this opposition was lifted and I was empowered from on high to soldier on with a new and confident peace in my heart."

Looking back on a pastoral ministry extending over a period of forty years in the Diocese of Cape Town, he tells me that the most moving and most memorable times were those spent on Robben Island and in the Pollsmoor Prison, sharing the Christian scriptures and celebrating the Eucharist with Nelson Mandela and other prominent political prisoners. "For me, being in Mandela's presence and just hearing him share his thoughts was like being with the warmest of friends. I often came away from those times together knowing I had been with a real child of God—a grown-up child of God."

When Harry and Jean bought their son David's house for their retirement, they decided to call it Dove Cottage because of the family crest. After moving in, they soon became aware that it lived up to its name. Every morning they wake up to the sound of a host of doves all cooing, with increasing volume: "Well done, South Africa! Well done, South Africa! Well done, South Africa!" they seem to say. Harry continues:

It is quite amazing what an effect this morning birdsong has had on us. The morning newspaper presents us with a constant picture of fraud and mismanagement in high places, with burgeoning crime statistics, stories of poverty, HIV/AIDS tragedies, and drug addiction disasters. But I am sure that, through the song of the morning doves, God reminds us that there is so much more that is good in our country that we ought to help people become aware of each day. I think of the huge blessing of having our country gifted with a Desmond Tutu and a Nelson Mandela, men with God-given vocations who have accepted great vulnerability through their single-minded love of all creation.

Vulnerability can come in many forms and without warning. When I was a young newspaper columnist, often profiling people who had triumphed over suffering, my father was suddenly taken ill. The previous weekend he and my mother had been cycling through the sunlit lanes of Thomas Hardy country. But the tints of fall were to change color dramatically. The sudden onset of his illness, the prognosis, and the subsequent desperation conspired into one long, dark winter. After a series of tests, a malignant brain tumor was diagnosed, and a consultant hinted that my father might not have long to live. It was hard to absorb and accept. After all, he had not reached his half century. As my father was suffering from terrific headaches and experiencing some difficulties with speech, surgeons decided to operate to release the pressure on his brain. I remember on one occasion, when my father was finding it particularly difficult to communicate, he struggled to form a word that was on his mind. It turned out to be "pigeons." I have often wondered why those birds were in his thoughts at that time. My father died a few weeks later. I have never forgotten how, at the very moment of his passing, our blue parakeet fluttered restlessly around its cage, flapping its wings and bursting into constant chatter and shrill. The sound from the cage was relentless.

Then a deep peace descended.

PART THREE
Living Flame

13

TOWARD THE STARS

See that I follow not the wrong path.
PSALM 139:24

As I watch the sun setting over the mountains, here on the northwest coast of Ireland, I can truthfully write that it has been an extraordinary day. Like the process of spiritual discernment itself, the art of journalism has something in common with criminal detection. Every story is a case, an investigation to be solved against the odds—and sometimes the published report, final broadcast, or ultimate course bears scant resemblance to the original idea. The path to finding the truth is usually paved with stumbling blocks. Contacts provide the clues but, until you hear or see it for yourself, there are never cast-iron guarantees that you are on the right trail. Even Agatha Christie's spinster sleuth, Miss Marple, noted for her brilliant deduction, can sometimes overlook the obvious: "Oh, I've been so stupid," she berates herself. "The missing element was staring me in the face." Whether it's clue-sniffing, journalistic investigation or spiritual searching, making the connection is vital. But it has to be the right connection—unveiling the extraordinary in the ordinary. Sometimes, though, the truth that lies closer to home can prove the most elusive. This is what I am discovering here on Ireland's north-south border where, as in the realm of vocation, things are not quite what they seem.

I never knew my only uncle, my father's older brother. He served with the coastal command of the Royal Air Force and was killed just before the end of the Second World War. When I visit the family grave, I always gaze at the inscription, "14th March 1945, aged 20." As a child, I would often look at his framed photograph and ask questions about how he had died so young. There had been little information about the accident. The plane on which he had been traveling had crashed near Enniskillen in County Fermanagh, Northern Ireland. Or so we had always thought.

All Souls' Day, when the church commemorates the dead, has always been an important time for me. Last autumn, while preparing for a trip to North America, I realized I would be away for the season of remembrance. So I decided to pack a small Bible in which I keep pictures of every member of the family. But, glancing through the photographs, I noticed that, for some reason, I didn't have one of Uncle Freddie. Rummaging through boxes of tiny black-and-white prints, I eventually located a picture of him, alongside his mother, and placed it at the front of the Bible. Somehow I had to have him with me on that trip, although I didn't know why.

That November 2, I found myself working in Canada. In the evening I decided to go to a Mass in the Newman chapel of the University of Toronto where a friend was celebrating that Eucharist. I took my uncle's picture along with me. It was a moving service. I was struck, in particular, by the words of one hymn: "We will run, for our God will be our strength and we will fly like the eagle, we will rise again."

My thoughts turned immediately to my uncle's gravestone, on which is carved an eagle with wings outspread, the Royal Air Force badge. Keen to bring home a copy of the hymn, I was told to speak to a nun. Noting her Irish accent, I asked where she was from. "Enniskillen," she replied. "What a coincidence," I rejoined. "My uncle died in an air crash near Enniskillen in 1945."

"I remember it," said the sister, much to my astonishment. "I was about twelve at the time. We were in school and
we heard it falling. We thought it had crashed into our roof.
The kids ducked down. It passed very quickly and crashed at
the Graan, in farmland belonging to a Passionist Monastery.
It missed the monastery building and the farm, then crashed
near trees."

The nun told me that she had thought it was an
American supplies plane. This didn't surprise me because the
family had always understood there was a North American
connection. She explained how, the following week, a group
of friends had gone to look at the wreckage. "I remember all
the silk parachutes lying unused across the field. There is a
memorial there now and a small monastery and nursing
home."

I was, to say the least, stunned that, on all days of the
year, I should meet, by chance, in Canada someone who
could apparently recall the crash in which my uncle had died
half a century before. Moreover, I was holding a photograph
of him as we chatted. Back home I informed my family all
about it and vowed one day to visit the site of the crash, now
that I knew there was a memorial. This is why I am in Ireland
today.

This morning I decide to call in at the local newspaper
office in Enniskillen, thinking their archives might reveal
more about the crash and that they might be able to publish
a short piece that might reunite me with some of the other
families who had lost relatives. I know from my own days as
a provincial journalist how this type of item often generates
copy for the correspondence columns.

The editor isn't around when I reach the office. So I ask
a colleague if she would like some details, and she suggests I
type up the facts on the computer screen. I have never liked
getting involved in stories about family and friends as it is
difficult to be objective—and it is certainly a strange experience bashing out copy about oneself. But on this occasion it

seems to save time and might also make a small contribution to the following week's diary column. A photographer then offers to drive me to the monastery where, we soon discover, there is a Marian grotto in memory of those who were killed that day. Before long, a priest is offering to say requiem prayers for Flight Sergeant Frederick Nicholas George Ford and all those who have died. I walk toward the grotto and bow my head.

Opening my eyes, I place red roses at the memorial as the photographer takes a succession of pictures, apologetically asking me to place the flowers for a second time so he can get a better shot. I haven't had time to study the epitaph but, as the camera clicks away and I reenact the tribute, my eyes suddenly catch sight of a date in the corner of the white marble. The memorial reads "14th May 1944," not "14th March 1945," the date on my uncle's grave. Perhaps there's been a mistake? Have I confused the dates? I mentioned my concerns to the photographer.

Meanwhile, the obliging priest digs out some wartime records from the monastic archives. As we talk, he begins to wonder what I am already suspecting: that my uncle actually died in another crash nearby. So strongly have I wanted to believe in the mysterious connection between my unknown uncle and the unknown sister in Canada that I have allowed myself to overlook the possibility that I might be on the wrong track. And the fact that the plane had come down in the shadow of a monastery has appealed both to my spiritual and journalistic instincts. There is a lesson here about the search for my true vocation and reading too much into certain situations.

Naturally I have to inform the newspaper office before the following week's edition but, by the time I manage to get hold of a member of the editorial team, she tells me that they had decided to run the original story straight away. Panic grips. Nobody mentioned the piece was destined for that night's print run; after all, it was hardly a "hold the front page" moment. "Don't worry. We won't say anything," they reassure me with echoes of the old journalistic—and Irish—adage about not letting the truth get in the way of a good story.

I appreciate their position but can't leave it there—and a more mysterious story begins to unfold as I resolve to find out what had really happened to my uncle's plane. With a friend as navigator, I set off from the monastery and drive back into Enniskillen to scan newspaper records on micro-fiche at the local library. But there is no mention of the crash because of wartime censorship. So we journey on to the local airport, St. Angelo, to inquire if my uncle was stationed there at any time. An air traffic controller directs us to Castle Archdale, one-time location of an RAF flying boat base, which had played a pivotal part in the Battle of the Atlantic, keeping Nazi U-boats at bay. Today it's a museum with visual displays, wartime music, military artifacts, and squadron notes. On one of the exhibition walls there, I noticed a sequence about RAF Coastal Command, the unit in which my uncle, an air gunner, served. The enlarged lettering dis-closes that the 201 Squadron had played a full part in the war against the U-boats and that alongside "the successes" had been several unfortunate accidents.

Consulting staff at the base, I am shown a book in which are listed the allied aircraft lost during the war. Studying the columns I come across the date 14th March 1945. Subsequent research verifies that Flight Sergeant Ford and eleven others, including a Canadian (the North American link), had tragically met their death that day. But not in Enniskillen as I had initially thought. A Sunderland Flying Boat, attached to the 201 Squadron, took off from Lower Lough Erne and crashed into Crownarad Mountain, above Fintra, northwest of Killybegs in County Donegal in the Republic of Ireland—nearly a two-hour drive away. I have to go there. A local historian puts me in touch with a man who has long had an interest in the flying boats of the

Second World War. Records show that the plane had indeed been on a U-boat mission to the Atlantic but at two-thirty in the morning had hit bad visibility and crashed above a small fishing town, bursting into flames as two of its four depth charges exploded.

I can't give up now. Storm clouds are gathering but the journey to Killybegs is one I have to undertake. Like a detective responding to a crucial tip-off, I head off at once, driving through some of Ireland's most beautiful scenery, over the border and along the coast. I keep thinking how all this physical searching mirrors my own spiritual quest. By mobile phone, we keep in touch with the guide who, from his home more than fifty miles away in Northern Ireland, gives me directions to the crash location as best he can.

Reaching the Killybegs area in a downpour, we travel on to a school at Fintra where we have been told to turn right, and "then left by a dump yard." I don't see a dump and wonder if we've missed it again. Then, after a close encounter with a truck full of sheep, I ask a local farmer about the site and he points up to the mountain, 1,700 feet above sea level. After negotiating a series of tortuous lanes and fielding further mobile phone calls, we eventually pull up beside a white tablet of stone with the letters "W. M." We think it must mean "War Memorial." But even then we are mistaken. W. M. stands for "Water Main." I can't get any closer because the actual site is nearly two miles up in the mountains. I need a guide. This evening, though, it seems that I am near enough. As I get out of the car, I can't help noticing a rainbow illuminating the brooding sky and yet, as I look up to the rocky terrain, where my uncle died, the sun is so powerful I can't see, the rays so overwhelming that I have to cover my eyes. Despite the sadness of the occasion, I experience it as a vision of hope and resurrection, the intersection of death and life. A dark day has turned into a light-filled evening, transfiguring the complexities of the journey into a holy encounter at dusk. I sense this is the place, but I feel also that I should venture no further, at least for the time being. This is sacred territory.

The traveling itself has seemed almost a parable of vocation: earthly pilgrimage itself is often honed from adventures, misunderstandings, errors—but always by the possibility of new horizons. Perhaps the light at the top of the mountain tonight appears only so radiant because of the difficulties and doubts that have emerged before. I learn that, for many years, a local priest has walked up to the crash site to say his prayers and remember the dead. The accident has become part of local history. On the fiftieth anniversary, some people from the town climbed to the site where wreckage still lies. Even though they had no connection with the crew and had never met the families, they did not want to forget and represented all those unknown relatives by taking part in a service.

My pilgrimage to Donegal today has been an eventful journey into the past, with chance encounters and assumptions, dead ends and detours. But ultimately it is one of light and eternity: a deeper sense of communion with the uncle I never knew. As day turns into night, I suddenly remember the Royal Air Force's Latin motto embossed on my uncle's grave: *Per ardua ad astra.*

Through endeavor to the stars.

14

BORDERLANDS

Borderlands are ambiguous places in which different cultures and traditions meet, frontiers from which the new can open up.

ESTHER DE WAAL

I'm studying a book called *Living on the Border of the Holy* (subtitled *Renewing the Priesthood of All*). The author, L. William Countryman, explains that the priesthood of the Christian people is lived out in the world of everyday existence. He notes that Jesus was not a priest of religion but allowed his nearness with God to be manifest in his living of everyday life. He reconnected the holy and the everyday in a way that gave reverence to the presence that was already there. He could see faith in God in the sick, hear truth in the words of a Gentile woman, and see the bountifulness of the creator "in the fleeting glory of wild flowers." In the preface Countryman states:

> By "priest" I mean any person who lives in the dangerous, exhilarating, life-giving borderlands of human existence, where the everyday experience of life opens up to reveal glimpses of the HOLY—and not only lives there but comes to the aid of others who are living there. The HOLY that the priest encounters in the borderlands is none other than

TRUTH, the TRUTH that underlies, permeates, upholds (and judges) us and our everyday world. It is remote and transcendent, and yet also as close and intimate as our own breath. The border where we encounter the HOLY is not just at the edge of our existence but, even more truly, at its center.[38]

This, then, is how my priesthood is being worked out—on the edge. I think the story in Luke's Gospel about the woman suffering from hemorrhages for twelve years has a particular meaning for those who find themselves on the margins. This woman of courage and faith comes up behind Jesus, being hemmed in by the crowds, and touches the fringe of his clothes. Immediately, her hemorrhaging stops. "Who touched me?" asks Jesus. "Someone touched me, for I noticed that power had gone out from me." When the woman realizes her identity cannot remain hidden, she comes toward him trembling and, falling down before him, declares in the presence of all the people why she has touched him and how she has been instantly healed. Jesus says to her, "Daughter, your faith has made you well. Go in peace." The power goes out from the fringe, from the hem of the garment, from the margins. Likewise in the Gospel of Matthew, we read of Christ ministering to the sick in Gennesaret. The people beg that "they might touch even the *fringe* of his cloak; and all who touched it were healed." Wholeness is bestowed from the edge.

Perhaps it does not therefore matter that I still find myself on the borders of Anglo- and Roman Catholicism. But it's important to bear in mind here that the opposite of Roman Catholic is not Protestant but sectarian because it breaks away from the whole. I want to be part of the whole. In my privileged work, I have an opportunity to meet the spiritual leaders of the day and sometimes, if there's time, I'm able to talk on a personal level with them. A Franciscan priest, Father Michael Seed, who has received many high-

profile people into the Roman Church, tells me that assisting
in one's pilgrimage of life or faith is the role of all the people
of God. He isn't talking about monopoly of faith or abso-
lutism but about personal growth and development and
authentic call. He thinks each of us is called to listen and to
inspire and to assist people in whatever way they feel God is
calling them to move. The meaning of conversion, he points
out, is, in a sense, a turning. To move on in one's pilgrimage,
there has to be an authentic prompting of the Holy Spirit.
There must be absolutely no sense of triumphalism and no
glamour. He goes on:

> I was brought up in the Salvation Army. I love it
> dearly. I am still Salvationist. I was raised in later
> life as an independent Baptist. I am still a Baptist.
> I don't give it up. It is with me. It is part of me. It
> is like a tree. If you look at the life of a tree, it's by
> the number of rings it has that we can know how
> old it is and what it went through. So it is with our
> bodies and our minds. I don't divest myself of or
> take off my Salvationist beauty any more than my
> Baptist beauty and now my Roman Catholic
> beauty—and indeed ugliness of all three. We're not
> exclusive. It's a development of our faith—that's
> the purpose of our life. It's development not stag-
> nation. And it isn't a sense of triumph. That is the
> way of the world. It isn't power. It's one's own per-
> sonal response to life and to God.

I still get nostalgic dreams about the Anglo–Catholic
church I grew up in. These memories are often set against
great streams of sunlight and feelings of resurrection.
Someone reminded me recently that Anglo-Catholicism
nourished me like my family—it formed my roots. And
they're bound to run deep. So when the opportunity arises to
interview the Benedictine writer Joan Chittister on the tele-

phone from Pennsylvania, I decide to put one or two questions of my own about nostalgia, a theme that has been preoccupying me for some time. Nostalgia, she declares, is destructive when it locks us into a spirituality that is an excuse for piety to become pietism and religion to become "a spiritual Jacuzzi." Nostalgia is about me and God, she says, a feel-good state that takes me back to home and mother. It's the smell of apple pie and the way things were. It's the bells, smells, and rituals. That's wonderful, she thinks, and it has a place but, when I am locked into that, I am not being called to the presence of God in all of life right now. If my holiness has to come from the past and cannot be in the present, then she doubts that is holiness at all.

At the same time, she thinks, there is a kind of nostalgia in spirituality that is absolutely essential: the memory of the best that we can be, that takes us all the way back in the Christian tradition, certainly to Jesus but also to the *abbas* and *ammas* in the desert, to the great spiritual figures in the years 200 and 300 who were trying to make sense of the great new insights and revelations they had been given. So when nostalgia arouses in us a memory of the past that catapults us into the future, and that enables us to live spiritually, morally, and well in the present, it is a marvelous tool, the bedrock of hope. But when nostalgia is an escape from the present and my fear of the future, it is not spirituality or religion. It becomes instead a psychological crutch, she believes.

I ask why she thinks nostalgia encircles my dreams. She says:

> You have to look at what the dream really was. The dream might show up in the form of a High Mass of childhood. You feel very good at it and it's so wonderful to be there. You wish you could have that spiritual life now because everything would be all right again. That's a kind of return-to-the-

womb dream. And I would have to ask myself
what is going on in my life now that makes it
essential or desirable for me to return to the
womb? What is it that I cannot face now? Where
is the loss in my spirituality now? It could be an
important dream all right, but I doubt very much
if it is about religion.

Today I interview a Catholic who grew up in Brazil
attending one Mass a year. The priests didn't have control, he
says, because there were none around. So the people did things.
He is someone who receives the sacrament in both Anglican
and Roman Catholic churches. I find his words inspiring:

> As a Christian you have to live with tensions. You
> have to make choices, and this gives you freedom.
> People who live according to what they are told to
> do are not free. If you embrace the tensions, you
> have constantly to make choices, to think about
> what you are doing. If you are told what to do and
> don't get out of that mindset, you don't think for
> yourself as a Christian. Our communion is our
> baptism, not the Eucharist. The Church has politi-
> cized the Eucharist and operated like an exclusive
> club, not a universal church.

It's the Feast of the Sacred Heart today, one of my
favorite times of the year. I have been reflecting on some
remarkable words of Karl Rahner, sent to me on a card:

The heart of Jesus
is God's heart in the world:

which collects into itself
our diversity and diversion:
in which, alone, the world discovers its mystery;
in which, alone, God becomes the heart
of our hearts; in which, alone, our
being finds its unified and
all-embracing center.

It is shortly after six in the morning. I light a candle in the prayer room after waking restlessly. The sun shines through the trees and in through the window. The rays come straight through the branches and appear to penetrate me. They light me up and pierce me. I have had dreams like this but now this is a blessing of radiance that is actually blinding me, the sun is so strong. It also purges me, staying with me for a minute through the wind-torn branches. Clouds build up and the sun vanishes. The rays disappear. I feel touched by God—totally unexpectedly—as if he "came down" to visit me in my prayer room, a sign of love and hidden glory.

I am woken up at twenty to four this morning by the sound of glorious birdsong, an opera solo from the branches I have never heard before. It is exquisite. Who is the bird? What is she singing? I first hear the notes in my dreams and think I'm in heaven because the music is so beautiful. Even now, at a quarter to eleven at night, the birds are chirping out there. What is their message for me?

A new song, perhaps?

15

VALLEY OF THE LAKES

What was the power that made me open out into this vast mystery like a bud in the forest at midnight!

RABINDRANATH TAGORE

We have moved into spring, and a journey through the twisting lanes of southern Ireland now finds me on the trail of a one-time "monastic city" whose ruins tell a story of their own. Whenever I'm in Ireland, I feel I'm walking on sacred territory. Even the trees and hillsides seem to radiate their own spiritual dynamic. The holy ground of Glendalough (which means valley of two lakes) has long been a place of restoration, especially for those who find institutional religion a stumbling block. The writer Esther de Waal describes this location in the Wicklow Mountains as "the place of resurrection" and I think I can see what she means. As I write, I hear the sound of birds and a rippling lake. Through my tired eyes, the shimmering light resembles hundreds of swallows fluttering their wings as they skim, like night-lights, over the darkening water. Around me are trees, rocks, bees, bracken, and yellow gorse. As Einstein put it, the most beautiful experience we can have is the mysterious.

The ancient roadway through the Wicklow Gap, marked by crosses and stones, has guided many a pilgrim over the mountains and down to this ancient Celtic site that once drew Christians from all over Europe. Two priests, Michael Rodgers (Roman Catholic) and Marcus Losack (Anglican), have set up an ecumenical retreat center here. "We came together from two different denominations and cultures, but shared the same basic faith and spiritual traditions," they say. "We see little sense in maintaining the divisions which fracture the visible unity of the churches." They met by accident in the Wicklows and, having settled in the area, now lead pilgrimages following in the footsteps of the *peregrini:* the pilgrims, wanderers, seekers, and exiles of Celtic times. As Esther de Waal writes:

> To be on pilgrimage is to move into a world where the dividing line between past and present, between this world and the next, between what we call sacred and what we call secular, dissolves. The outward journey is also a journey inwards. We have to be prepared to let go of the accustomed patterns and controls that we impose on our daily lives, and instead be ready to be open to what lies beyond—and what is most often expressed in symbol, image and poetry.[39]

Glendalough may have been a religious center before the arrival of Christianity in Ireland in the fourth century. A classic example of an early Celtic monastery, it is a liminal place where, according to the notes in front of me, "the veil between this world and the next was perceived to be only wafer thin."[40]

Although encouraged by his parents to follow a religious path—an angel is said to have appeared to his pregnant mother and informed her that her son would be "dear to both God and man...and the father over many monks"—St. Kevin had his own early sense of calling. While still young, he escaped from the monastery he had joined and hid in the mountains. Eventually he came to Glendalough and made his way to the upper lake where he could be alone and pray. He lived out his austerity in the hollow of a tree, living on herbs and water. They say he stayed there for many days until a cow, brought to graze in the area, began to lick his garments. The daily ritual is said to have resulted in vast quantities of milk. Herdsmen eventually unearthed Kevin's hideaway and he was taken back to the monastery.

For all these romantic tales, Kevin seems also to have faced inner turmoil over his extreme religious fervor and his commitment to remain celibate. One unflattering story, associated with his monastic training, reveals how a young girl spied him in the fields with his brethren and fell passionately in love. But Kevin resisted. One day, discovering him alone, she embraced him and asked him to lie with her. Mortified, Kevin ran off and rolled naked in a bed of stinging nettles. He looked up to find the love-struck girl following in pursuit. So he took a bunch of nettles and began to beat her around the face, hands, and feet. Falling on her knees, she begged his forgiveness, promising to dedicate her life to God by becoming a nun. Vocations are clearly galvanized by many different circumstances.

As well as being a hermit, ascetic, and Christian mystic, Kevin was apparently a noted performer of miracles, drawing inspiration from the spiritual tradition of the Desert Fathers. His cell was on the dark side of the lake, remaining in shadow for six months of the year. He wrote poetry and prose, devised a Rule for monks in Irish verse, and relaxed by playing the harp. He was also a gentle individual, with an extraordinary affinity with nature and a spontaneous love of animals and birds. One childhood tale describes how a white cow came to his parents' house every morning and evening with milk for Kevin. In Irish mythology, the cow is sacred, and one proverb talks of the animal as "one of the pleasant trees of paradise." In Irish folk tradition, milk is a source of poetry and the cow a symbol of wisdom and brightness, qualities attributed also to Kevin.

One Lent, St. Kevin fled the company of his monks, as was his custom at that time of year, and went in search of greater solitude. Finding a small hut to protect him from the elements, he spent time alone, reading and praying in deep contemplation. He would often pray "the cross vigil," which involved standing or kneeling for long periods in the shape of a cross (the sacred tree). One day, while praying with his arms outstretched through the window of his cell, a blackbird came and made a nest in his hand. Kevin kept silence and continued his prayers, not wanting to disturb the bird. He remained completely still until she had hatched her eggs. In a woodcarving of the saint, sculptor Imogen Stuart depicts an old man sitting on the ground with bare feet, holding the bird in his hand.

One story describes how wild beasts from the woods and mountains would come and drink from the saint's hands. Another relates how a huntsman once entered the valley, following his dogs that were chasing a wild boar. The beast ran into Kevin's oratory, but the dogs were frightened off their scent and lay down before the door. Kevin remained praying beneath the trees while birds perched on his head and shoulders. They flew around him warbling "sweet hymns in honor of God's servant." The hunter then called away his dogs because of the reverence he felt toward the anchorite.

A famous legend has it that Kevin prayed for an hour every night in the cold waters of the lake where a monster used to try to distract him by curling itself around his body, then biting and stinging him. Another tells how he banished a monster from the Lower Lake to the Upper Lake where he lived alone, effectively taking the monster to himself. It is said that the fervor of his prayer, his patience, and the fire of God's love in him rendered the monster harmless. As the guidebook authors comment, "We all fight the 'monsters of the deep'; we all struggle with conflicts and contradictory longings that pull us at times in different directions."[41]

As I absorb these words, I apply them to myself. And here at Glendalough I hear the song of the nightingale again.

The calling is being redefined right here on the edge of the lake and the edge of eternity. This, I sense, is an ecumenical vocation to write and reconcile. As I make my way through the arched gateway, past the tall round tower and into the former cathedral, I sense again that this is a place where the transcendent and immanent are intertwined. Using the priests' book as a guide, I wander through the ruins and onto a path that leads to the upper lake. There I look out across the still, glistening water and imagine St. Kevin practicing his ascetic exercises; praying for an hour every night in the cold waters is a chilling thought. At this point the guidebook recommends something far less arduous but perhaps equally powerful. Pick up a stone, it says, to represent the demons in your life, the guilt and failures, the wounds and frustrations. Cast it into the lake as a symbolic act of letting go. So I find a stone and onto it project my burdens. I throw it northwards. It skims the surface and drowns. Have my sorrows gone with it? I notice the lake is soon calm again after being disturbed.

I listen to the birdsong and eye the shafts of light that penetrate the water. The book tells me to expect a range of colors at different times of the day. I walk back along the shore and head over a stile toward a ledge of rock. This is St. Kevin's cell, once a beehive made with stones. So this is where the saintly loner, clad in animal skins, would have given spiritual guidance to his visitors. What remains today are a few foundation stones lying in a half circle with three oak trees growing up around, but to me it still seems sacred, close to earth and heaven. And standing in that cell I think about the barriers that keep the Christian churches apart— the rules, suspicions, and disagreements—the road blocks on the path to unity. I wonder what lies ahead, when we shall be able to share an authentic sense of togetherness. There are certainly many signs of hope around and I sense that, within the Celtic tradition of healing, further inspiration can be drawn. Then, quite suddenly, I find myself stretching out my arms in the shape of a cross as St. Kevin might have done fourteen centuries before. In contemplating the future, in the spirit of the past, I discover the sanctity of the present moment.

The shadows are lengthening and it's time to return but, as I start to retrace my steps, I glance back at the stretch of water and wonder what secrets it holds. Then it dawns that something distinctly mysterious has happened. The silent lake has become for me, not so much a symbol, but a sacrament of communion where the wounds of religious apartheid can perhaps finally be laid to rest. Here I resolve to enter more deeply into my vocation. After several years with the BBC's religion and ethics department, I sense a calling to a more reflective way of life. I have to get the equilibrium right. I will give up my job again and work in an independent capacity. This will enable me still to broadcast but also give me time to write books and undertake more academic work in theology, something that has been beckoning for a while. I need to create that balance in order to become more deeply the person God intends me to be. My journalism and my theology must synthesize on a more spiritual plane now.

I am being called toward my uniqueness.

16

VIGIL AT DUSK

My soul pines away with grief.
PSALM 119:28

I see the wintry sun setting over the salt marshes as I turn left from the country lane and drive on to a smoother stretch of road. After watching the car ahead shrink into the twilight, I find myself in darkness. I have been journeying for about a minute when, all of a sudden, I notice a rabbit on the roadside, in particular its lively eyes. They seem attracted to the headlights and the young animal approaches. Then, thud…and thud. I screech to a halt, the only driver on the road. Although an indescribable sense of guilt and responsibility kicks in, I know there is nothing I could have done to avoid the creature. In shock, I reverse the car. Then, through my rearview mirror, I focus on a motionless bundle of fur lying in the middle of the road. One minute life, the next death. It is a distressing sight, especially for an animal-lover with a rabbit of his own as a family pet.

Fast cars come and go, so I reverse into a gateway, wincing as, one by one, the vehicles pass over the body. Opening the trunk, I take out a towel, once given to me by Indian pilgrims at Taizé. It has had many uses over the years; now it is to become a shroud. I run down to the rabbit and lift its warm body onto the cloth, covering the body as tenderly as I can before the next car rushes by. Then, tearfully, I scramble into a field and slosh about in the mud, trying to locate an appropriate spot to place the corpse. Holding the vulnerable creature close to my breast, I repeatedly tell it I am so sorry. It is a pitiful episode—just me and a poor dead rabbit on a dark, bleak night beside a wood.

As I climb onto the wall separating field from forest, I get caught in some barbed wire and stumble back. A deer runs off in fright. I hear an owl in the distance, while birds from the wood complete their own evensong. I clamber over fences, hedges, and brambles to return the rabbit to its habitat. There I notice a wooden crate sunk into the ground. I place the creature under the crate. Its little gray legs keep popping out of the towel and there is blood by the nose. The rabbit is now lying on its side with one open eye penetrating mine. It reminds me of an eye of Christ, painted on an icon back home, hundreds of miles away, and of those eyes on the Swedish altar. I keep thinking of Mary cradling the body of Jesus at the foot of the cross—and of St. Francis whose delight in touching animals enabled him to make friends with a range of creatures including rabbits and a hare.

I cover the bundle in leaves and place three large stones beside the crate. I say some spontaneous prayers in the night sky. Alongside this rabbit against the moonlit sky, I know I am involved in a spiritual encounter hard to articulate. The mystery deepens when I subsequently learn that the locals haven't seen a rabbit in the locality for several years; they have all been wiped out by myxomatosis, an infectious viral disease that has obliterated an entire animal population. A villager later informs me: "There aren't any around here anymore."

The experience both unnerves and exhilarates. Despite the melancholy and distress, I know I am enfolded in an unconditional love, an experience of union I can describe only as mystery. I feel at a crossroads. As the Episcopal theologian L. William Countryman explains:

The border country where we encounter GOD at the limits of our everyday experience is a frightening place. It has about it an element of death—death, at least, to the ordinary and predictable, if not always death in the most literal sense. When we find ourselves on this boundary, we are in a place of decision and danger. Even if we believe GOD is a GOD who has loved us and given us gifts, who has reached out to us across whatever separates us, it is still a challenge to look toward the future, to let go of our anxieties, and to live actively in the assurance that GOD, when all is said and done, will continue to love and commune and work with us. The HIDDEN HOLY is neither against us nor aloof from us, but *for* us (Romans 8:31).[42]

At the same time the experience opens my eyes to the rhythms of nature as I attune my senses to its smells and sounds. I have so many dreams about animals, always set in radiant landscapes and eternal sunlight. The darkness has been vanquished. Wounds have been healed. Vulnerability has been redeemed.

There, in the shadow of the glen, I connect my own vulnerability to that of the rabbit. I begin to understand a little more about the vulnerability of God. Only such a God could be strong enough to take on the world's pain and die on a cross, a love that could give—and continues to give—itself. As a professor of philosophy and religion comments: "Trust in such a God can give human beings the strength to risk following on the path of compassion and vulnerability, to think what it means to live lives whose first priority is love."[43]

I continue to reflect on the experience. Whatever I might previously have understood by *vocation*, I begin to discern a distinctly divine pattern in the way in which my own spiritual journey has been shaped by other people's pain, both professionally and personally. Moreover, it occurs to me that these different worlds have never been separate but are all of a piece. However much I might want to distinguish between the role I am playing and who I really am as a person, the truth is that both identities are starting to merge. Perhaps I am called not only to be vulnerable as a friend but vulnerable as a reporter too. In a profession noted for detachment, objectivity, and resilience, this is not an attribute I would readily proclaim from the rooftops. But I have to admit to myself in the privacy of these pages that, however motivated I have been to get to the truth of a particular story, I have always felt a spiritual connection with the suffering I am reporting on, far more powerful than the assignment itself. It is not so much empathy, more a visceral compassion, just as I might feel at the bedside of a dying friend, hovering between two worlds in the twilight hours. These are intriguing times for me.

But there is a more personal reason for the sadness I feel that day. At home we have our own silver lop rabbit, which lives most of his time indoors and is the tamest of pets. Fully domesticated, with a character of his own, Lucien has taught us much about love, vulnerability—even gender: for the first few months he was Lucy, until the vet took a closer look. He sprawls out in front of the fire like an elongated doorstop but can change shape at a moment's notice. Although he often positions himself on the borderline of rooms and flower beds, his favorite haunt is the hearth, sitting on the cool tiles with sphinxlike stillness. While he doesn't like to be elevated or carried, he is naturally affectionate and responds to human attention for long periods at any time of the day. His hourly ablutions are a work of art, and his disciplined way of life means that, every evening at twenty to eleven, he gets up and moves toward bed—a straw and hay dormitory all to himself in the garage. Lucien also feels pain. Although he hardly makes a sound when investigating the secrets of the great herbaceous outdoors, he occasionally stumbles across a stone, hurts a paw, and heals it with his tongue. We always know when he is unwell. He resorts to a corner of the room, puffs himself into a ball tight to the baseboard, and sits brooding for hours.

I've heard a workman ask if he's real, a question reminiscent of the children's classic *The Velveteen Rabbit* that speaks to me about love, pain, death, and resurrection. One day a toy rabbit asks: "What is REAL? Does it mean having things which buzz inside you and a stick-out handle?" The Skin Horse replies, "Real isn't how you are made. It's a thing that happens to you. When a child loves you for a long, long time, not just to play with, but REALLY loves you, then you become Real." The rabbit is curious: "Does it hurt?" The Skin Horse wisely admits, "Sometimes. When you are Real you don't mind being hurt."[44]

Through Lucien I have learnt much about vulnerability, reality, and beauty—effectively about becoming alive. His systematic sniffing out of every flower and shrub reminds me to be more conscious of the sacred sensuousness around me, to be open and alert to the natural environment, to see the extraordinary in the ordinary. There is also something reassuring about his presence. He's great company, even though he never utters a word. I have often heard it said that stroking fur is therapeutic, but there may be even more to it than that. According to a clinical psychologist at a London hospital, the visit of pets, including rabbits, to children's wards can give a sense of security. Children find spells in a hospital alienating. They experience medical staff "taking something from them," and they often become wary and withdrawn. Animals on the ward provide an opportunity for sick children to take control, if only for the duration of the visit. The animals make them feel safe and special, enhancing their self-esteem in a strange environment. The children feel they are "looking after" rather than "being looked after." A rabbit was the only creature one terminally ill child wanted to touch before she slipped into a coma and died.

Intriguing, therefore, that a famous Christian healing sanctuary, hidden in a Welsh valley, has associations with both a saint and a hare. This place of pilgrimage dates to the seventh century. In the church at Pennant Melangell, near Llangynog, in the Anglican diocese of St. Asaph, lies the oldest surviving Romanesque shrine in the United Kingdom. Its history involves hares. A young Irish woman, Melangell, the daughter of a Celtic prince, abandoned her life in Ireland and came to Britain. She had a distinct sense of divine vocation but desired also to escape a marriage that was being arranged for her. Eventually Melangell discovered a place of silence and prayer in a lone valley in the Berwyns. One day the local prince was out hunting with horses and dogs and, as the guide book, puts it:

> The wild animals of the district scatter before him. As he rides up the valley he urges his hounds on to follow a hare which has escaped into a thicket. There in the thicket he finds not only the hare but also a young woman, evidently a woman of prayer, who is sheltering the hare under the hem of her garment. He urges on the dogs; they withdraw in fright; his huntsman lifts his horn to his lips; his hands and his horn stick fast. Before the holiness, the simplicity, the directness of the virgin, the martial arts of the young chieftain become as it were paralyzed. According to the legend, the prince and the maiden speak. She tells him her story and he accepts the reality of her unusual calling. He promises not only to give her land in the valley but that hares will always find protection there. It has been supposed that Melangell offered him the assurance and protection of her prayers. The prince rode on but Melangell remained, creating a religious community. The wild hares ran in and out among them as if they were their pets.[45]

After St. Melangell's death, her grave became a place of healing and sanctuary for women and men in distress as well as for hunted animals. For post-Reformation Christians, fearful of acknowledging their devotion to the Virgin Mary or of using her name, the hare became a secret Marian symbol, woven into tapestries or carved into wood, in much the same way as the fish became the emblem for persecuted believers in the early Christian centuries. Today, close to the church at Pennant Melangell, a cancer treatment center attracts many patients and pilgrimage groups. The administrator comments, "Time seems to stand still and a sense of balance and of being part of God's created world calms...one is drawn into a thin place between heaven and earth and the sense of God's presence."

...Back in the Scottish wood, nursing the warm body of the rabbit, something has happened, and its meaning is still unfolding. As Julian of Norwich observes: "Here I saw a great unity between Christ and us, as I understand it; for when he was in pain we were in pain, and all creatures able to suffer pain suffered with him."[46] As swiftly as the death itself, I have become mysteriously bonded to the animal whose life I have taken. In the sadness of the hour, I feel deep reverence for the mysteries of the natural world. With the moon moving between the branches of the silent forest, I stand respectfully beside the sylvan sepulcher and feel at one with the universe.

This is sacred ground.

17

SWAN SONG

In your house, I am a passing guest,
a pilgrim, like all my fathers
PSALM 39:12

*A*fter a relentless spell of writing, I have made my
way to the small Benedictine monastery of Christ
our Savior for a short retreat in the heart of the English
countryside. It is here that I feel in touch with the particularity and unpredictability of vocation. My biography on Henri
Nouwen, published two years ago, has opened up an unex-
pected ministry to those who find themselves on the edge of
the church. A biography of the first victim of 9/11, the New
York fire chaplain and Franciscan friar, Father Mychal
Judge, is about to roll from the presses. Others are in the
pipeline. But I need to put other people's stories to one side
for a while. This is a time to pause on my pilgrimage and rest.

The converted barn in the village of Turvey, Bedford-
shire, is the home of five monks. They share the offices and
meals with a twin community of nuns who live nearby in a
grand old house. I am warmly welcomed and shown to the
guest quarters, a converted stable, where I am introduced to
a short, bald-headed man called Ralph, who has known conversion himself. Hospitable and loquacious, he serves lunch,
then politely asks if he can talk to me over the meal.
Although I have fled the world of deadlines for silence, I

instinctively know this is someone with a story to tell. Within minutes, I learn he was jailed for armed robbery, has been in twenty-seven prisons, and even shot a gangster who torched his flat "to black ash, the color of your shirt. It would have been life if I'd killed him as I'd intended." He tells me he has also been an alcoholic as well as a cocaine and heroin addict.

My eating utensils are at this point suspended between the plate and my mouth. Then Ralph goes on to describe how he had a life-transforming encounter with an archangel, was taken on as an oblate, and hopes one day to become a monk. I stop eating altogether. Even though I am not really in a journalistic mode, my curiosity gets the better of me and I start to ask questions, revealing in the process what I do for a living. Ralph beams with delight. From then on, my stay is punctuated with graphic descriptions of his dramatic, and sometimes violent, past. "If you want to write my story, you would be very welcome, and I will help you all I can," he tells me proudly. But it isn't merely Ralph's criminal exploits that grab my attention. I detect also that Ralph is a sincere and prayerful man of deep conviction. Strange, when I see him wearing his white oblate's robe in the chapel, I can visualize him also in prison uniform. He tells me that listening in his cell to a religious service, broadcast on BBC radio, was the catalyst for his conversion.

We keep in touch by e-mail for a while. "What I told you is so very true and a wonderful blessing for my life," he writes. "God bless you and keep you safe and may His holy angels surround and protect you always. Receive all my love and friendship. Br. Ralph. Obl. OSB."

I then receive a letter from one of the brothers, informing me that Ralph has died but, in his final weeks, fulfilled his dream and was professed as a monk. I reread the prayers he sent me and feel I have to return to the monastery to hear more about his extraordinary life—and death. There is much to learn from his story about the uniqueness of vocation and about dreams being fulfilled before the end of one's life.

On a return visit to Turvey, I am discovering from the monks how Ralph's search for love and security began very early in life. His father died before he was born. His father died before he was born. Ralph, a twin, was the only child in the family to be sent to an orphanage and didn't come back until he was ten. As a teenager he went to sea, serving both in the Merchant Navy and Royal Navy. He wed and had children, but his marriage broke up. Then, shortly after leaving the Navy, his mother died in front of him as she was peeling potatoes. This succession of setbacks led Ralph to the bottle, and for the next eighteen months he became a vagabond, drifting in and out of work. Then he turned to crime, spending a total of fourteen years in jail—eight of them for double armed robbery. In his mid-forties he robbed a rent office at gunpoint twice in two weeks—the second time, he went back shouting "Rebate!" As an inmate, he knew the temptations of drugs, drink, and porn, but prison life also offered opportunities: he passed an A-level in English literature and undertook computer literacy courses.

Then, on January 1, 1997, Ralph underwent a series of life-transforming experiences, including a visitation, he maintained, by the archangel Michael. A figure had appeared him and a "weird light" had surrounded him. Over a two-week period, he experienced a number of visions as well as dreams featuring the Blessed Virgin Mary and the pope. He had been terrified but was nonetheless at peace. He interpreted the apparitions as an invitation to religious conversion. An Anglican by upbringing, he went to an evangelical service in prison, but found the atmosphere too brash. So he decided to attend a Roman Catholic Mass and felt immediately at home. He later developed a particular devotion to the Virgin Mary and said he could not imagine a family without a mother. Guided by the Catholic prison chaplain, he was received into the Catholic Church and never looked back. Inmates nicknamed him "The Monk" because of the religious kitsch that accumulated in his cell—glow-in-the-dark statues of Mary, snowflake models of the ascension, and holograms of Thérèse of Lisieux. For him these were not idols but prompts to prayer. He read the Bible dutifully and enrolled in a course in catechetics.

"He had a sense of the faith that was natural to him somehow," recalls Brother Tom Ward. "He sensed, knew, or felt very strongly about the real presence in the Eucharist and the doctrines about Our Lady. This was part of the package Ralph had been given. Then someone sent him a book called *Christ's Call to the Monastery*. He never knew who but, as he had a keen sense of providence and the supernatural, he discerned it as a call from God to enter a monastery."

As his release date drew near, Ralph had small cards printed: on one side was an illustration of the Eucharist, on the other his name and address. He drew up a resumé, located a Catholic directory, and started writing off to monasteries asking for a job. He explained that he didn't want money because he had a small Navy pension; all he desired was a room and a bowl of broth at the end of the day. Many of the monasteries he contacted responded cautiously, but Dom Gregory van der Kleij, the superior at Christ our Savior Monastery, decided he would take Ralph on for a trial period.

When Brother Herbert Kaden and Brother John Mayhead collected Ralph from a café near the prison, they were surprised to find him smartly dressed in a black suit with his shorn hair resembling a tonsure. As a prisoner, Ralph had known the world of confinement and had grown accustomed to the rhythms of enclosed life—the monastic environment wouldn't come as too much of a shock. He knew how a small room could take on a special character and become a home.

But, more than anything, he longed for the monastery to be a more caring community than prison, and he imagined his new inmates would show love toward him all the time. "He thought there wouldn't be the sort of tensions he had found in jail, but there were those tensions here, and I know Ralph found that initially very difficult," says Brother Tom. "He had lived in different sorts of closed institutions all his life. The small monastery here is less structured than many. He may have been looking for a more structured way of life."

The new venture was clearly a risk both for Ralph and the community. Although devoted to its prayer life and eager to please everyone, Ralph could be garrulous, noisy, and melodramatic. The monks soon realized he would be too loud for the monastery building itself, so he was asked to look after the guest house, which he kept scrupulously clean and tidy. It was important, though, for him to have a specific role, so he arranged to have white smocks made to show he was "half a monk." He even designed a badge with the words "Guest House Manager," which the brothers considered inappropriate. Ralph was keen to share the story of his conversion with all who visited. Some guests found him overpowering and occasionally curtailed their retreats. Others loved to hear his tales, and close friendships were formed. But beneath the bravado lurked a raw vulnerability. Brother Herbert recalled the day the superior told Ralph that he had passed his probationary period and could stay at the monastery:

> He danced around the room exclaiming, "I've got a home! I've got a home." It was so moving I could weep now; it was so beautiful. I think he enriched the community. While it wasn't always easy for him or for us, he got milder in his behavior and less exaggerated. We saw the humility of the man forming and, from the beginning, if he annoyed one of us, he would always come and apologize. He never bore malice.

It was natural for Ralph, searching for love and security, to feel fully part of community life. "He wanted to be in the monastery forever and never be sent away again," Brother Tom tells me. "He was part of a close community that was going to care for him. But he also felt called by God to become a monk. It would have been a great sorrow for him if he hadn't become a monk."

However, Ralph's journey into the fullness of Benedictine monasticism was to take him through a dark vale. He had some health problems and, during the spring and early summer of 2002, he started to lose weight. One morning last August, he awoke with stomach pains and looked jaundiced. An emergency hospital admission led to tests that revealed he was suffering from terminal cancer. The nature of his illness was kept secret from him because he had always been petrified of such a diagnosis. He was allowed to return to the monastery where he learned he had only a short time to live. Dom Gregory decided it was appropriate that Ralph should become a monk before he died.

"It had never been ruled out," says Brother Tom, explaining further:

> He was seriously committed to monastic life. He had lived through a period of disillusionment and had stuck with it. I think, in the very long term, we would have been open to his eventually becoming a monk. But when someone's dying, you have to make decisions about what's appropriate then. There was a very real God-given call for him to be a monk. There are various tests which St. Benedict gives in his Rule about whether you should let someone persevere in the monastic life. One is whether they can put up with harsh words—which Ralph could. Another is whether they genuinely seek God—which he did. A further test is whether they have obedience, which Ralph did, and a

fourth is whether they are faithful to the office—
Ralph hated missing prayers, even if we'd asked
him to look after guests instead. Having said that,
accepting harsh words and obedience did not come
easily to Ralph. But he didn't lose heart and, eventually, was always prepared to admit when he was
wrong. His life was structured around the commu-
nal prayer of the Office and his own private saying
of the Rosary and studying the Bible. That was the
center of his life.

In view of the little time left, however, Ralph had to be
fast-tracked. Because he was not as tall as his fellow
brethren, none of the community's habits would fit, so one
had to be swiftly borrowed from a shorter monk at another
monastery. The service of profession took place in the chapel,
but because Ralph was so weak, he had to make his life vows
sitting in a chair. Brother Tom tells me:

> Three times he had to say the words "Sustain me
> Lord according to your promise and I shall live. Do
> not disappoint me in my hope." It was poignant
> and joyful but also sad because we knew Ralph
> would not live. Normally a prospective monk is a
> postulant for nine months and a novice for at least
> a year, then he makes simple vows for three years
> and after that his solemn vows. Ralph did the lot in
> one day and became Brother Michael.

The former armed robber was a monk for just twelve
days. Determined to have a habit of his own, Brother Michael
asked the same woman who had designed his smocks to come
and a make a garment he knew would cover his body at death.
As the illness took its toll, physically and mentally, Ralph
struggled to the chapel to say his prayers. But he also loved the
theatre of it and would give blessings to visitors as he passed.

"He addressed the whole of his dying with a tremendous dignity, courage, and real faith," says Brother Tom.

As the new monk became progressively weaker, a hospice nurse between jobs moved in on a voluntary basis to supervise his dying. He still loved to receive visitors and, increasingly, prayer became the focus of his life, even though he found the practice of it more and more difficult. When it was impossible for him to join the community for the Offices, he would say the Rosary from his bed and the brothers would pray with him. It was sad, however, to see him forget the words of the Hail Mary as he had always loved saying the Rosary. He wanted to be part of the community to the end. On his last day, the atmosphere at Turvey seemed to quiet. Brother Michael was incapable of moving or responding a great deal, so the nuns and monks continued to pray with him. At about 6 p.m. on Thursday, September 12, his breathing slowed and, with the community saying psalms around the bed, the new brother died. Bright sunlight streamed through the windows and the hens he had looked after so faithfully seemed to cluck with greater vigor. Brother Tom reflects further on his life:

> This was a man whose life was profoundly and genuinely changed, yet whose flaws and vulnerabilities stayed with him, which meant he had to live his Christian faith in a monastery with real courage and determination. He didn't fit in entirely comfortably, certainly to begin with, but the mark of his real goodness and genuineness was that he stuck with it. He worked with grace as it confronted him again and again. He experienced a real Christian conversion. It was deep and it was sincere.
>
> I think at one level Ralph loved his story and telling people about it. There was also something sadder because, at some level, I don't think he could stop regarding himself as a criminal. There was the

time when an opportunist thief stole money from the monastery. Ralph couldn't get out of his head the suspicion that we would think it was him, which no one did for a minute. The only person who regarded Ralph as a thief here was Ralph. I don't think he could let go of that. A few days before he died, when he was muddled, he heard a radio report about a local bank robbery. He was convinced people would think it was him. It was very important for him to know that he was loved and that people didn't think of him as a crook or armed robber, even though he loved the drama of the life he had led.

The last weeks were "a tremendous experience" for the community as their newly professed brother accepted his death with a mixture of acceptance and sadness. During his last supper with them, Brother Michael told the superior, "Dom Gregory, I love you." Those words of gratitude brought tears to the eyes of all around the table. Deprived of so much as a child, Brother Michael had spent a lifetime searching for a sense of belonging. There at Turvey he had found a home at last, and his monastic family noticed significant changes within him over the time he spent with them. "And the community has grown through the experience too," Brother Herbert tells me. "I think Ralph had been a very lonely person, but here he found his freedom and discovered how he could be loved by so many different people."

The monk adds: "One always grows through strange and moving experiences."

18

SACRED PATTERNS

Day unto day takes up the story
And night unto night makes known the message
PSALM 19:2

*L*ast year, on the feast of St. Francis de Sales, patron saint of writers, a Benedictine monk gave me a special blessing. I had wanted to make a public recommitment to my vocation and it seemed an appropriate day. Since the benediction, fourteen months ago, spiritual writing seems to have become a ministry, connecting me with people on the edge. I sense I am moving into the person God created me to be.

I am now in Madrid to research a new biography. It is the day of the state funeral of those killed in the city's commuter train bombings. Candles are burning in the city's churches. Last night I was stopped and searched by secret police hunting the Moroccan suspects. A man approached me and asked for directions. I happened to be carrying a black bag. Before I had time to focus my eyes on his map, we were both pounced on from the shadows and told to hand over our documents and bank notes. The man turned out to be Moroccan and officers had been on his trail. Inadvertently, I became part of the antiterrorist operation.

I recall that, after the attacks on the twin towers in New York in September 2001, Osama bin Laden stated that mass murder on such a scale avenged a number of old scores with the West. These included the ousting of the Muslim emirs of al-Andalus from Spain in 1492. Spain was therefore on al-Qaeda's hit list, not only because of the war in Iraq, but because certain Islamists maintain that any land that was once part of the Muslim fold should always remain under Muslim rule.

This morning I met a Catholic priest. We got chatting to him about the vulnerability of life and its impact on our callings. "I like the point of knowing that I am vulnerable—that bad things don't just happen to other people," he commented, and then explained:

> I can no longer think terrorism is for others, like the people of New York, and not for me. Vulnerability is no longer a theoretical issue but a practical one. Two days before the Madrid attacks, at the same hour, I was in the Atocha railway station, so the bombings have made me think. This bringing home of vulnerability to me has been healthy, a positive development. I had been hiding from myself the fact that things like this could happen to me. Now I realize they can happen to anyone. I am vulnerable. I am perishable. I am old already, so anything can happen to me any day. The realization of that was welcome. The essence of life for me is to take whatever comes to me, good or bad, risks or dangers. I like to take risks curiously. I think that risks make me come alive. I think there is a line of Shakespeare about security being man's worst enemy. God has taken a risk with me. He is enjoying it, and I am enjoying it too.

The priest acknowledged that the call of God could sometimes come through darkness. "The dark night of the soul" was an expression dear to any Spaniard's heart since childhood. The bombings had been like that. The priest

recalled a Spanish poet who once wrote about looking at the
sky. The poet was asked which cluster told him more—the
faraway beautiful white clouds or the dark clouds coming
close to earth and bringing with them rain. The dark clouds,
according to the poet, was how God had come closer to him.
"That idea is true," the priest continued, saying:

> The darkness may occasionally bring God closer to
> us. But I don't like the idea of a vulnerable God,
> although I realize it is a very useful topic for mod-
> ern theologians: the idea of an omnipotent, arbi-
> trary God versus a compassionate God in
> solidarity with human suffering. To say that if God
> is vulnerable he suffers somehow upsets my
> schemes. I am hoping to go to heaven and to be
> happy with God in heaven. If I reach heaven and
> find that God is not happy and is suffering, I won-
> der what I will do.
>
> The calling of God is a total calling—both to joy
> and to suffering. Both are unavoidable. If we desire
> solely one dimension, we need also the other. I
> wouldn't say that the calling brings the suffering
> by itself, though. The calling brings both. One of
> my spiritual teachers used to make the comparison
> of childbirth. First comes the joy of husband and
> wife conceiving—the greatest pleasure on earth—
> and then come the doubts, the anxieties, and the
> suffering of childbirth. Both are needed—the joy
> and the suffering—to bring out the new being, the
> new birth.

Now I am making the slow, two-hour train journey
north of Madrid. I know that the Moorish presence across
Spain over eight hundred years is an essential feature of its

history. Articles I'm reading in the carriage confirm it. "The castles and the palaces that are studded across the Spanish peninsula, and which now serve as the key tourist attractions of many a Castilian plain, were built by Arabs and Spaniards alike during their long struggle for control..." The Muslim civilization in Spain had been "rich, sophisticated and scholarly, and the Christians had learnt much from it. Indeed, in many respects it was more sophisticated and tolerant than the early Christianity of that period. Jews and indeed Christians were tolerated in the Muslim midst...provided they paid their taxes."[47]

Through the Guadarrama Mountains, I journey on to the medieval walled city Segovia in the region of Castile, 3,280 feet above sea level. Its fortress, the Alcazar castle, was a source of inspiration to Walt Disney. This is also where Queen Isabel promised Columbus the financial backing he needed to sail to America. The city is noted for its world-renowned Roman aqueduct, the largest and best preserved of its kind anywhere. Less well-publicized is Segovia's connection with the sixteenth century mystic St. John of the Cross. Within the walled city I notice a street named after him and an imposing statue. There are also other fascinating religious influences. I walked past a bar calling itself *El Purgatorio* and a restaurant known as *La Concepcion*. Hanging above a café in the main square is a white poster with large black lettering: *SOLIDARIDAD CON LAS VICTIMAS DE MADRID.*

As I wander through the city, I trace the strands of St. John's vocation. Born in 1542, he entered the Carmelite order at the age of twenty-one, taking the name St. John of Matthias. He studied in Salamanca and was ordained in 1567. That same year, he met Teresa of Avila, who persuaded him to collaborate in the reform of the order. On November 11, 1568, he changed his name to St. John of the Cross, assumed the Primitive Rule, and helped found the first monastery of the reform. He subsequently became rector of the college at Alcala and confessor of the Carmelite nuns in

Avila where Teresa was prioress. John was kidnapped by Carmelites hostile to the form and was harshly treated during imprisonment in Toledo where he began to write his greatest poetry. He managed to escape, continuing to write mystical poems and compose lengthy commentaries inspired by his Scholastic theological training.

John came to Segovia for the first time with Teresa in 1574. He served as superior of the Carmelite monastery here from 1588 to 1591. It was then a city of around 18,000 inhabitants and the hub of a flourishing wool and textile industry. It was the mystic's home for all but the last few months of his life when he underwent further persecution. In his last years, he was involved in a ministry of spiritual direction, managed the internal affairs of the order, and extended and rebuilt the monastery. The monastery is set outside the city walls with impressive views across the river of the Alcazar towering above. One can see, says the local guide sheet, "exactly where Fray Juan acquired additional land, how he moved the buildings away from the river, and built a garden under the cliffs which marked the new boundary. The route up into the city is the one he took on his visits to confess the Discalced nuns, established there since 1574."

Here in Segovia I've been meeting Spanish composer and poet Óscar Muñoz who describes himself as a "modern mystic." He has set to music many mystical texts including St. John of the Cross's *Spiritual Canticle*. "St. John never pretended to be a poet but he is considered the best Spanish poet," Óscar tells me.

> [St. John] represents the idea of forgetting your own plans and letting your soul, your inner being, speak and manifest itself. It is like the discovery of light shining on the water, a lyrical moment of

abandoning yourself in the world. The veils covering us are so dense that the spiritual dimensions of life are needed more and more. I think music, poetry, and myth are the means of liberating ourselves from our restrictions and conditioning and bringing us back to the sacred. The artist is like a shaman who connects the depths of the human soul with the divine world.

Óscar considers the language of St. John so simple and unpretentious that the poet is able to awaken something in the reader, reconnecting that person with a world waiting to be observed and listened to. Even though I studied the writings of St. John two decades ago, as an undergraduate, I now feel the poet has something further to teach me about my own vocation and the art of letting go. Vocation is about freedom, not burden, I surmise. Moreover, it can never be completely understood, not in this life. As Óscar explains:

I am a modern mystic in the sense that I can't stop looking at or looking for the mysterious or the numinous—that which is here but which does not reveal itself completely. St. John of the Cross talks in terms of "Where did you go beloved, leaving me alone in this state?" You see it, then you miss it. You want it more, but it escapes and fades away. I have had some sort of minor connections with divinity through meditation and through music, but it is so difficult to talk about it. It is very private. Somehow if I talk about what happened directly, I betray something that happened in those moments. The best way to talk about these things is through art, through a musician's notes or an artist's brush strokes. There is a need to express it and give thanks for it through a shared creativity.

But you don't have to name it. Somehow if you
name it, you lose it.

As someone who has written and broadcast so often
about other people's journeys and experiences, these words
remind me that there are boundaries, even (perhaps especially) for a journalist of the spiritual. A natural inclination
to write down, photograph, record, and communicate needs
to be kept in check when reflecting on matters of the sacred.

As I walk onto the Carmelite monastery grounds, I
notice quotations from St. John's *The Living Flame of Love,*
a poem that guides us to the gentleness of the inner life of
God. Inside the church my eyes are drawn to a remarkable
altarpiece representing the literary works of St. John. At its
height is the *Ascent of Mount Carmel,* a shrouded mountain
where only the glory of God abides; at the base in blue is a
spring of living water hidden in the divine manna; to the left,
a depiction of the dark night; and to the right, a living flame.
The centerpiece is a statue of Our Lady of Mount Carmel,
"the synthesis of perfection."

Friars who knew John only by reputation were afraid to
live with him because they presumed he would be a harsh
and uncompromising superior who would force them to
undergo unthinkable penances. But when they moved in
alongside, they observed a very different man. John would
often take them out for days on the hillsides to bask in the
beauties of nature and was known for his affectionate and
compassionate care of the sick. In fact, in his younger days,
he almost became a hospital chaplain. Vocation should
always be characterized by humility and gentleness, not
ambition and power. In a short commentary on the gentleness of the saint, the American Catholic priest Thomas Cane
writes about the choices we all have to make in our lives,
especially when we are trying to discern the voice—and the
way—of God:

When we come to a decision...we try to discern what is his will, and make it our own. It is this very process that becomes the threshing floor of our hearts. We make a good decision, faithful to our commitment to follow Jesus in all things; we get accustomed to it; and then circumstances beyond our control so alter the situation that the decision has to be gone through again. This happens time after time. We struggle with God's will; give ourselves over to it; and the other side of that surrender has an experience of insight and serenity that frees us to go out to others with new vitality and simplicity. Then the situation is changed and we are once again thrown back into discernment.

As this becomes a distinct pattern in our lives we come to recognize that something of great importance is taking place and that the revelation of what God is doing here will come as a gift in the deep silence of prayer, not in talking it over, or thinking it through on our own, though both of those have their place. Eventually the silence discloses its secret.[48]

After his death, the body of John of the Cross lay in the ancient chapel of Carmel until his beatification in 1675. The remains are now encased in a large urn on top of a grand sepulcher. As I saunter into the deep silence of the chamber, I think back to my university days studying the writings of St. John. I kneel on the marble, praying for my family, friends, guides, and tutors who have helped me gain a deeper understanding of my vocation which, increasingly, is centered on writing about and caring for people on the edge. As my mind falls quiet here in Segovia and I become lost in the silence, a pigeon starts to coo in an arch above a window. It continues for some minutes and then its song of welcome fades. A journey through the dark night of calling is being transfigured. I feel at one and alone with God and, through the interplay of light and shadows, rejoice in a unique relationship. I sense this experience is propelling me toward the truth of my calling, although I do not fully understand it. I leave the monastery and head back to the walled city.

I continue to fathom what it might mean.

CADENZA

The beasts and trees will one day share with us a new creation and we will see them as God sees them and know that they are very good.

THOMAS MERTON

A western journalist once visited the Dalai Lama, taking with him a tape recorder. Fifteen minutes into the interview, the Dalai Lama leaned across and pressed the *Stop* button. He explained to the baffled correspondent that an ant had just crawled into the recorder and, if it continued running, the mechanism could crush and kill the insect. The exiled spiritual leader of Tibet insisted the conversation be suspended until the ant emerged from the machine. In the meantime, they should refrain from talking. Three hours later, oblivious of the impending deadline, the tiny creature emerged from its submechanical exploration. The *Record* button was duly pressed again and the interview resumed. In Buddhism, all of life is sacred, the Dalai Lama told the reporter.

There were no straying insects on the table when, a few months after returning from Segovia, it was my turn to interview the Dalai Lama. In any case, these days we use mini discrecorders, which are much harder to infiltrate. For some reason, I have always felt that I could not retire from journalism until I had met the Dalai Lama! And today I did. A disarming figure with an infectious chuckle, the world's most famous Buddhist teacher struck me as a most remarkable spiritual figure whose views on the interconnectedness of the whole of creation helped me even further to make sense of my vocation. "My approach to promote such human values as compassion and affection is worked out, not through religious tradition, but through awareness," he told me. "To take care of yourself—in order to gain maximum benefit for yourself—you need a close relationship with other human beings, with animals, and with the environment. I think anyone can be transformed into a warm-hearted person if they are long-sighted in their awareness."

Among the media entourage in Scotland's capital, Edinburgh, were members of a production team making a "fly on the wall" documentary about the Dalai Lama in honor of his seventieth birthday in June 2005. They've been following His Holiness around the world and seem much impressed by his deep-rooted interest in the environment that emerges in many of his talks. The positive energy one gives to the environment reflects one's own well-being, the Dalai Lama believes. One's personal happiness is contingent on how one treats animals and the environment. To feel at one with creation is the secret. Using the paradigm of the family life of apes, the Dalai Lama underlines the importance of a mother's love for her child. Young primates who cuddle up to their mothers often become much more successful in groups and less prone to destructive behavior.

As I reflected later on these insights, I glanced across at an array of newspaper headlines about people who seemed to be living by an entirely different standard.

A hunt was underway for a gang whose "sadistic attack" on an injured swan was thought to have hastened her death and doomed her unborn cygnets. The swan, already weakened by infection after sitting on her nest during floods, had become the victim of a ferocious attack. Youths had hurled a skateboard and a milk crate at the defenseless creature before stoning and abusing her as she tried to protect her eggs. Animal rescue officers took the swan to a treatment center where she died a few days later. Her mate and six young cygnets were left dismayed and disoriented as they searched in vain for the missing swan up and down the river.

In a separate story, four boys were being questioned by police after a group of children broke into a zoo and kicked a baby wallaby to death. After attacking the two-month-old animal, they threw it into a pool where it drowned. They then dragged the body out of the water and slung it back into the enclosure. Other members of the wallaby family were reported to be "obviously distressed."

Four drunken soldiers, returning from an alcoholic spree, stamped on a hedgehog crossing the road and used its body as a football. "It was a barbaric attack on a completely defenseless and harmless creature," a resident was quoted as saying. "They were laughing and swearing while they were kicking it around. It was horrific."

An "overweight thug" was facing prison after he drop-kicked a kitten twelve feet over a washing line "like a rugby ball." He booted the three-month-old kitten so forcefully that the animal's back was broken.

And owners of a garden center (which sells birdhouses, feeders, and seeds) were refusing to explain why they brought in a hit man to kill a family of robins nesting under their roof. According to the manager, the robins were flying into the restaurant, but staff told reporters that the robins had merely triggered a new intruder alarm that was keeping their boss awake at night.

These twenty-first-century acts of animal cruelty and contempt for our fellow creatures could not be more at variance with the seventh-century theology of St. Isaac the Syrian who defines "a compassionate heart" as one "on fire for the whole of creation, for humanity, for the birds, for the animals, for demons, and for all that exists." When confronted by the pain and anguish of any living thing, a person with such a heart will shed many tears. "As a result of this deep mercy his heart shrinks and cannot bear to look on any injury or the slightest suffering of any in creation."[49] Likewise, the twelfth-century theologian St. Bonaventure (who wrote a biography of St. Francis of Assisi) urges Christians to deepen their awareness of the divine gift of creation:

> The creatures of the sense world signify *the invisible attributes of God,* partly because God is the origin, exemplar and end of every creature, and every effect is the sign of its cause, the exemplification of its exemplar and the path to the end, to which it leads....For every creature is by its nature a kind of effigy and likeness of the eternal Wisdom....
>
> Therefore, open your eyes, alert the ears of your spirit, open your lips and apply your heart so that in all creatures you may see, hear, praise, love and worship, glorify and honor your God lest the whole world rise up against you.[50]

I first read these lines as an intellectual exercise while I was studying theology at the university, but now they speak to me at a deeper, personal level. I have even had vivid dreams about creation, lit in the brightest Technicolor. In one sequence, all the flowers and animals blessed and touched me. It was extraordinary. I was walking in Franciscan sandals and felt connected to the whole of creation.

As I record these thoughts, I am grieving for a much-loved family pet whose recent death has brought my calling into sharper definition. Timothy, a pink-eared, bushy-tailed chinchilla—a rodent with ancestral roots in the Andes—had an extraordinary presence, bonding in a unique way with the rabbit Lucien, with whom he developed a close relationship. Tim was an adventure-loving rascal who made the most of his freedom. For many years he lived in my brother's house where he disappeared into cavities, escaped out of windows, gnawed books, and once walked off with a burning cigar. A nocturnal creature, he possessed all the instincts of a mountaineer with a head for heights and a penchant for risk-taking. Defying death on several occasions, he even made local headlines for his domestic acrobatics.

Then, one year, my brother brought him to the family home for Christmas. There, Tim introduced himself to Lucien, with whom he soon struck up a deep rapport. Admittedly, the rabbit was a little suspicious at first but, after a while, he and the chinchilla formed an attachment that both touched us and taught us. They were inseparable, offering care and affection at every turn. And we, in turn, learned much about the nature of unconditional love. Every night they would lie together for hours in spontaneous displays of complete trust and love. Friends and neighbors would look on in astonishment as the pair positioned themselves in front of fire and remained there as living symbols of loyalty and faith. Then Tim became ill and died within a few days. Moreover, it was Lucien's birthday, a reminder that death and life are often intertwined. When I learned the news in the middle of a recording, the interview was hard to resume. But then I realized I could not have been in a more appropriate building: a church dedicated to St. Francis of Assisi.

We all felt the parting of Timothy acutely. It was at the level of mystery. Lucien retreated to corners and started to lose his alacrity. He stopped eating, lost weight, and simply closed his eyes, attentive to his own pain. So still and silent was his presence, we thought we might lose him too. During those sad weeks, we embraced each other's vulnerability. As the theologian Andrew Linzey explains:

> Anyone who has shared his or her life with a companion animal will know the terrible sense of loss occasioned by its death. Such is the reality of the human-animal bond that the experience of bereavement can be as deep, sometimes even

deeper, than the loss of another human subject. Christian theology has simply failed to recognize both the spiritual significance of animal-human companionship and the sense of spiritual desolation bequeathed by its loss.[51]

As we lowered the small casket into the ground, I remember spontaneously exclaiming that this nine-and-a-half-year-old animal had brought not only joy into our lives but had also shown us how to love. Indeed, a friend observed at the time: "When Tim and Lucien were together, they possessed their own distinctive personalities. They just tried to be themselves. They didn't try to be anything other than themselves. There were symbols of unconditional love."

The gift of empathy with the whole of creation is wonderful (full-of-wonder)—but costly too, my spiritual director reminded me. However, taking on the pain was worth the price. Bereavement was an especially deep wound when it concerned creatures who depended on us and relied on our love. She continued:

> Two totally unique creatures bonding with each other is indeed a sign of what might be possible if only we could "see" with the eyes of God and love with the power of the Spirit. Each of these lovely creatures has been part of your family, and the shared grief is likewise a sharing in the journey for each of you. We are meant to have a deep attachment to other creatures. Somehow your own vulnerability is exactly the gift bestowed on you so that you can speak on behalf of others—all God's creatures in the Franciscan sense. It would have been a tragic mistake had you avoided staying with the pain and mystery of the little chinchilla's death. He was God's messenger and was surely with you and the family, including the rabbit, for a reason—

and often such explanations are revealed only much later.

I am ruminating on her words this evening as sparrows and wood pigeons flutter between the conifers and a black-bird directs its orange beak toward nuts and husks on the ground. In front of a cotoneaster bush, shielding a panoply of blooms, is a bronze statue of St. Francis, looking down on Tim's resting place. Some days Lucien comes and sits among the flowers that now bloom over the grave. Catherine of Siena wisely points out that "the reason why God's servants love his creatures so deeply is that they realize how deeply Christ loves them. And it is the very character of love to love what is loved by those we love." And, according to the priest Thomas Berry, the religious traditions "need to awaken again to the natural world as the primary manifestation of the divine to human intelligence." He goes on:

> The very nature and purpose of the human is to experience this intimate presence that comes to us through natural phenomena. Such is the purpose of having eyes and ears and feeling sensitivity, and all our other senses. We have no inner spiritual development without outer experience. Immediately, when we see or experience any natural phenomenon, when we see a flower, a butterfly, a tree, when we feel the evening breeze flow over us or wade in a stream of clear water, our natural response is immediate, intuitive, transforming, ecstatic. Everywhere we find ourselves invaded by the world of the sacred.[52]

Similar observations by the American monk and writer Wayne Teasdale are important to note. He remembers walking through a monastic garden in upstate New York and hearing the prior remark that "flowers are a contemplation in which God is expressing his love for us." Later, "contemplating over time" a rosebush in his front yard in West Hartford, Connecticut, Teasdale concludes that, like the rose, reality is a process of growth or unfolding. Just as the rose is more than any one stage of its development—bud, stem, or bloom—so life and reality are more than any one moment of time or experience. Vocation, I believe, is like that too. What is real, Teasdale senses, is not just the flower's moments of duration but also the totality of the process in its manifestation in time:

> This insight can comfort us in facing death and disintegration. All nature communicates this truth to us all the time, if we would but pay attention—the attention of the heart, of intuition, of our being to the sacred mystery. Nature constantly teaches us that a larger picture exists than what we see. It compels us to awaken by confronting us with order, design, and perfection everywhere.
>
> A spider weaving its web, the perfect symmetry of a snowflake, the beauty and harmony of the lily, the cosmic quality of trees, the mysterious presence of the wind, the attraction of stillness, the radiance of light, the transparency of fragrances, the flow of water, the movement of leaves, the timeless feeling of some days and nights, the poetry of birds in flight, the transfiguring moments of dawn and sunset, the hypnotic rhythm of the tides—all speak to us of something beyond ourselves, something that transcends our understanding. All point to nature's ability to nourish us aesthetically and psychologically as well as materially.[53]

Retracing the course of my spiritual pilgrimage through eight volumes of journaling, I have begun to discern a pattern, a process even, though much remains hidden. I realize how, in the search for our true calling, we may at times be drawn, understandably, in different directions. We may feel compelled, or at least obliged, to follow a certain path, deafened even by a myriad of voices recommending a route that may not be a divine direction at all. Indeed, we may rank pleasing others above making our own decisions and blossoming into our true selves. We may even desire to become like those we most admire.

Reliving these journal entries, I have wondered if there are any divine blueprints, as such, after all. What seems more conclusive is that, in the very claiming of our uniqueness and difference, God is both sought and found—and this is at the root of spiritual ambiguity and paradox. All that is desired is that we trustingly receive and accept our originality, our defining individuality, from the heart of a self-giving God. In the words of Elizabeth Canham:

> Growth in self-knowledge teaches us that we are a glorious, ragbag collection of motivations, beliefs and insecurities. At times we are people of courage with our faith firmly rooted in God, but we are also subject to fear and uncertainty. We wrestle inwardly with our inconsistency and the contradictoriness of so much of life. The journal enables us to say "Yes, I am this" while I acknowledge that I am also "that," and in the present time the two do not seem reconcilable. I consent to live with ambiguity and to celebrate the wonder of God's grace which constantly supplies me with the strength to be and to become.[54]

All my life I have been a traveler—journalistically, spiritually, and psychologically—and I am feeling called to novel landscapes as I write. But for all my wanderings and wonderings, for all the woods and thickets, mountains and shorelines, for all the wounds and the blessings of love (which will doubtless continue as the journey moves on), I have discovered at least this: The mystery of divine calling lies much closer to home than we might suspect, its extraordinary secrets hidden in the ordinary events of our lives. Moreover, it is nature itself that holds the key to a more profound understanding of who we were created to be. In my own case, it was the presence of two vulnerable creatures, intimately bonded, but also distinctly themselves, that enabled me, finally, to claim the uniqueness of my own vocation—to stay close to the edge of the forest and listen more attentively to the new songs coming from the trees.

Everything drew me to love and thank God;
people, trees, plants, animals—I saw them all
as my kinsfold...

From THE WAY OF A PILGRIM

ACKNOWLEDGMENTS

*A*lthough my name appears on the front cover of this book, there are many who have worked less prominently behind the scenes to ensure its smooth publication. I should like to thank Father Lawrence Boadt, publisher at Paulist Press, for giving his blessing to this project; to managing editor Paul McMahon for his patient encouragement and professionalism; and to Barbara McCormick, Jill Gleichman, Lynn Else, and Susan Heyboer O'Keefe. Closer to home, special thanks to my mother, Margaret, and brother, Nigel; and to Ainsley Griffiths, Eva Heymann, Lee Humphreys, Peter Huxham, Jerry Kilby, Bill Kirkpatrick, Teresa Malone, Tim Pike, May Spearing, John Squire, Ernie and Doreen Webber; to Tom Jordan, editor of *Spirituality*; to film makers Joshua Dugdale and Jonathan Jenkins; and to Harry and Jean Wiggett in South Africa for their support. David Torevell read the draft meticulously and made helpful comments. Last, but not least, my gratitude to Timothy and Lucien whose friendship unlocked the meaning of this story.

NOTES

While the author and Paulist Press have endeavored to complete these references with as much data as possible, there may be some omissions, owing to the fact that the quotations were copied into private journals not originally intended for publications.

1. Gregory Collins, OSB, *The Glenstal Book of Icons* (Blackrock, Ireland: The Columba Press, 2002), 46.

2. Joa Bolendas, as quoted by Gregory Collins, 47.

3. Ibid., 44–45.

4. Cyprian Smith, *The Way of Paradox: Spiritual Life as Taught by Meister Eckhart* (London: Darton, Longman and Todd, 1987), 27.

5. Elizabeth Canham, *Journaling with Jeremiah* (Mahwah, NJ: Paulist Press, 1992), 105.

6. Sister Wendy Beckett, *The Mystery of Love* (London: HarperCollins*Religious*, 1996), 2.

7. From *Birds of Britain*, The Monthly Web Magazine for Birdwatchers, http://www.birdsofbritain.co.uk/.

8. Stanzas 34 through 39 of *The Spiritual Canticle*, in *St. John of the Cross, Selected Writings*, edited with an introduction by Kieran Kavanaugh, OCD, The Classics of Western Spirituality (New York/Mahwah, NJ: Paulist Press, 1987), 226–27.

9. The *Collected Works of St. John of the Cross*, translated by Kieran Kavanaugh, OCD, and Otilio Rodriguez, OCD (Washington, DC: ICS Publications, 1979), 560.

10. Maggie Ross, *Pillars of Flame: Power, Priesthood, and Spiritual Maturity* (London: SCM Press Ltd., undated), 17.

11. Henri J. M. Nouwen, *Reaching Out: The Three Movements of the Spiritual Life* (London: Fount Paperbacks, 1980), 16.

12. Paul Murray, *A Journey with Jonah: The Spirituality of Bewilderment* (Blackrock, Ireland: The Columba Press, 2002), 61.

13. Canham, *Journaling with Jeremiah,* 3.

14. Dietrich Bonhoeffer, *Letters and Papers from Prison* (London: SCM Press, 1968), 173.

15. Stanza 14, *Spiritual Canticle.*

16. George Every et al., *The Time of the Spirit* (Crestwood, NY: St. Vladimir's Seminary Press, 1984), 54.

17. Quoted in William Elliott, *Tying Rocks to Clouds* (New York: Image Books, 1995), 246–47.

18. Rowan Williams, *Silence and Honey Cakes* (Oxford: Lion Publishing, 2003), 106–7.

19. Pierre Solignac, *The Christian Neurosis* (London: SCM Press, 1982), 164.

20. Quoted in Steven Chase, *Comtemplation and Compassion* (London: Darton, Longman and Todd Ltd, 2003), 93.

21. Una Kroll, *Crossing Boundaries in Prayer* (Norwich, UK: The Canterbury Press Norwich, 2000), 10.

22. Anthony Bloom, *Meditations on a Theme* (London/New York: Continuum 2003), 26–27.

23. St. Bonaventure, *Major Life of St. Francis,* Ch. VIII, No. 9, as quoted in *The Message of St. Francis* (New York: Penguin Studio, 1998), 30.

24. *The Little Flowers of St. Francis of Assisi,* edited and adapted from a translation by W. Heywood (New York: Vintage Spiritual Classics, 1998), 36–37.

25. Henri J. M. Nouwen, Donald P. McNeill, and Douglas Morrison, *Compassion* (London: Darton, Longman and Todd Ltd, 1987), 65.

26. Rembert G. Weakland, in *Being a Priest Today,* ed. Donald J. Goergen (Collegeville, MN: The Liturgical Press, 1992), 182 ff.

27. Gerald Priestland, *The Dilemmas of Journalism* (Guildford and London: Lutterworth Press, 1979), 114.

28. David Steindl-Rast, *The Music of Silence: Entering the Sacred Space of Monastic Experience* (San Francisco: HarperSanFrancisco, 1995), 5.

29. Ibid., 27.

30. Esther de Waal, *Seeking God* (London: HarperCollins-Religious, 1996), 76 and 78.

31. Recounted by Parker J. Palmer in *The Promise of Paradox* (Notre Dame, IN: Ave Maria Press, 1980), 46–47.

32. From *Against the Heathen* 42:3, 27.

33. St. Ephrem the Syrian, *Faith 18:6*, quoted by Sebastian Brock, *The Luminous Eye: The Spiritual World Vision of St. Ephrem the Syrian* (Kalamazoo, MI: Cistercian Publications, 1992), 59.

34. Pope John Paul II, *Redemptor Hominis*, 15.

35. Henri J. M. Nouwen, *Bread for the Journey: Reflections for Every Day of the Year* (London: Darton, Longman and Todd Ltd, 1996), 11.

36. For further reading, see Thomas Merton, *When the Trees Say Nothing*, edited by Kathleen Deignan (Notre Dame, IN: Sorin Books, 2003).

37. This particular poem of Harry Wiggett has been published only as part of a private collection.

38. L. William Countryman, *Living on the Border of the Holy: Renewing the Priesthood of All* (Harrisburg, PA: Morehouse Publishing 1999), xi.

39. Esther de Waal, Foreword to *Glendalough: A Celtic Pilgrimage,* by Michael Rodgers and Marcus Losack (Blackrock, Ireland: The Columba Press, 1996), 9.

40. Rodgers and Losack, *Glendalough,* 39.

41. Ibid., 16–28.

42. Countryman, *Living on the Border of the Holy,* 186.

43. William C. Placher, *Narratives of a Vulnerable God* (Louisville, KY: Westminster John Knox Press), 1994, 21.

44. Margery Williams, *The Velveteen Rabbit* (New York: Puffin Books, 1995), 14–15.

45. A. M. Allchin, *Pennant Melangell: Place of Pilgrimage* (Powys, North Wales: Gwasg Santes Melangell, 1994), 5.

46. Julian of Norwich, *Showings,* translated with an introduction by Edmund Colledge, OSA, and James Walsh, SJ (New York/Ramsey, NJ: Paulist Press, 1978), 210.

47. Isabella Thomas, "The Queen and the Moors," *The Tablet* (London), March 20, 2004, 6.

48. Thomas Kane, *Gentleness in St. John of the Cross* (Oxford: SLG Press, 1999), 12–13.

49. As quoted by Hilarion Alfeyev, *The Spiritual World of Isaac the Syrian* (Kalamazoo, MI: Cistercian Publications, 2000), 9.

50. Bonaventure, *The Soul's Journey into God*, chapter 2, par. 12. The second paragraph of the quote may be from an unknown source.

51. Andrew Linzey, *Animal Rites: Liturgies of Animal Care* (London: SCM Press, 1999), 109.

52. Thomas Berry in the foreword to Merton's *When the Trees Say Nothing*, 17–18.

53. Wayne Teasdale, *A Monk in the World* (Novato, CA: New World Library, 2002), 7–8.

54. Canham, *Journaling with Jeremiah*, 5.